◆ The ◆ Casablanca Companion

The Movie and More

JEFF SIEGEL

TAYLOR PUBLISHING COMPANY
DALLAS • TEXAS

PUBLISHED BY

TAYLOR PUBLISHING COMPANY

1550 West Mockingbird Lane

Dallas, Texas 75235

PHOTOGRAPHS FROM

THE EVERETT COLLECTION,

BISON ARCHIVES,

THE BETTMANN ARCHIVE,

THE MEMORY SHOP,

MOVIE STAR NEWS

and the author's collection.

DESIGNED BY LURELLE CHEVERIE

LIBRARY OF CONGRESS CATALOGING-IN-PUBLICATION DATA

Siegel, Jeff, 1958–
    The Casablanca companion : the movie and more / Jeff
Siegel.
        p. cm.
    Includes index.
    ISBN 0-87833-796-2 : $9.95
    1. Casablanca (Motion picture) I. Title.
PN1997.C3523S57—1992   91-46776
791.43'72—dc20   CIP

PRINTED IN THE UNITED STATES OF AMERICA
10 9 8 7 6 5 4 3 2 1

9/8/9~

B7- 91

◆ The ◆
Casablanca
Companion

TO LYNNE

Acknowledgments

No one writes a book by themselves, especially a book such as this. I owe so much to so many, including countless public relations people, that it is impossible to list them all. To them I offer my thanks. This book would not have been possible without the help of Lee Murray, who is not only a good friend but knows more about making movies than any film school graduate. Murray Burnett let me ask him the same silly, stupid questions thousands of interviewers have asked him over the past fifty years. Marianne Lampke of the Brattle Theater had more important things to do than talk to me, but found time anyway. Jim Donovan and Holly McGuire at Taylor Publishing are the best examples of editors I know.

◆ Contents ◆

ACKNOWLEDGMENTS vi

INTRODUCTION 1

1 ◆ THE STORY ◆ 4

2 ◆THE PLAYERS ◆ 27

3 ◆ WHO WROTE *CASABLANCA?* ◆ 66

4 ◆ THE FANS, THE CRITICS,
AND THE UNCONVERTED ◆ 93

5 ◆ THE IMITATORS ◆ 111

6 ◆ FOR THE TRUE
CASABLANQUISTE ◆ 135

INDEX 148

RAINS, HENREID, BERGMAN, AND BOGART

POSE FOR A PUBLICITY STILL.

Introduction

*W*hen I was in college, I met a woman who had never seen *Casablanca*. I was stunned that anyone could have led such a sheltered existence.

I, on the other hand, had already seen the movie so many times that I could recite the dialogue verbatim—and I was only twenty or so. Watching Humphrey Bogart beat his fist against the table in the "Play it again, Sam" scene seemed not only cinematically correct, but part of an entirely natural and acceptable way to order your life—you run guns to the Ethiopians, drink bourbon when your heart is broken, and shoot as many Nazis as possible.

I'm older now, but my view of the world still includes much of what I learned from watching the story of three people over two days in a saloon in French North Africa. And that, I'm sure, goes a long way toward explaining why *Casablanca* is even more popular today, fifty years after it was released, than ever before.

If one movie defines how Americans think of themselves, it's *Casablanca*. The film shows us as we want to be—cynical yet idealistic, independent yet romantic, worldly yet naive. How many of us fervently want to believe that we would have made the same choices Bogart did, from fighting the fascists in Spain to opening a popular nightclub to wearing a dinner jacket the way it's made to be worn? The rest of the world might think of Westerns or gangster pictures when they think of the United States, but Americans will always define themselves by

"AS TIME GOES BY. . . ."

Casablanca. This goes a long way toward explaining why no one has remade the picture; if its vision is already sublime, anything else would only be a disappointment. Yes, parts of it are silly and sappy, but I'm sure that millions besides me are perfectly prepared to explain why

Rick Blaine's behavior is sensible, logical, and morally correct. This is something that many of the film's critics (and even its admirers) miss. Its message applies today just as it did in 1942, when the Axis powers controlled most of the world that wasn't the United States.

For *Casablanca* is, as much as anything else, a morality play. At the risk of reading too much into a product of the American mass media/pop culture industry (made by the same Hollywood studio system, after all, that gave us such immortal memories as Ma and Pa Kettle and Esther Williams musicals), it's safe to say that the film—perhaps more than anything else to ever come out of Hollywood—outlines a view of the world that is as American as the Declaration of Independence. We are the good guys, says *Casablanca*, and if we don't lose sight of our goal and are prepared to work hard and to make sacrifices to achieve it, we can make the world a better place—not just for us, but for everyone, scumbag Nazis included.

One
The Story

*J*ngrid Bergman's Hollywood career had started splendidly in 1939, when producer David O. Selznick brought her from Sweden to make *Intermezzo* with Leslie Howard. But in the next three years, she made three flops, and despite glowing reviews for her and for one of the prettiest faces in the industry, she couldn't get a part.

Much of this inactivity was Selznick's fault. He owned Bergman's contract and, in Hollywood's old studio days, that meant she could do nothing unless Selznick wanted her to do it. Selznick, basking in the glow of *Gone With the Wind*, was perfectly content to let Bergman stew, occasionally selling her services to the highest bidder and keeping most of the proceeds himself. That's why Bergman made stinkers such as *Rage in Heaven* and *Dr. Jekyll and Mr. Hyde* (which, starring Bergman, Spencer Tracy, and Lana Turner and directed by *GWTW*'s Victor Fleming, is a candidate for the worst movie ever made by people who should have known better).

Bergman was furious with Selznick. "I never thought I should be able to say these things about David, whom I liked very much. But times change," she wrote to a friend during that interlude. She wondered if she would ever make a movie again, or would be forced to retire to Rochester, New York, where her husband was a dental student, her career over at the age of twenty-five.

Bergman shouldn't have worried. Selznick's behavior was notorious (he had pulled similar stunts with Alfred Hitchcock and Vivien

Leigh), and it didn't detract from her ability, which was well known at the other major studios.

In early 1941, Bergman got a phone call from Selznick. He told her he was thinking about lending her to Warner Bros. for a part in a movie about a saloon keeper in North Africa. "I don't know quite what the

UGARTE: "YOU DESPISE ME, DON'T YOU?"

RICK: "WELL, IF I GAVE IT ANY THOUGHT,
I PROBABLY WOULD."

RICK: "I DON'T BUY OR SELL HUMAN BEINGS."
FERRARI: "THAT'S TOO BAD.
THAT'S CASABLANCA'S LEADING COMMODITY."

story is," he said, "but I'm so glad you are going to be beautifully dressed and you are going to have a beautiful entrance."

Warners, however, wanted Bergman to do more than wear pretty clothing. Hal B. Wallis, the movie's producer, wanted Bergman—and only Bergman—for the female lead in their saloon keeper picture. "She was," said Wallis, the head of production at the studio, "the only actress with the luminous quality, the warmth and tenderness for the role."

The film needed something, for it had not fared well up to that point in early 1942. Warners executives couldn't even agree on whether to make an "A" or "B" picture, which in those days was the first thing decided about every film. A "B" picture was made quickly with a second-string cast on a cheap budget (see any Abbott and Costello movie); an "A" picture had a couple of stars (at least), and featured a schedule and budget with room for more than one camera angle for each scene.

This indecision made Warners' disagreements about whom to cast, which director to hire, and what to put in the script seem pointless. In fact, two sets of writers had been working on the script for six weeks, and had turned out little that was usable. In one draft, the hero was an American lawyer who had deserted his wife and children—hardly the kind of material that showed up in Hollywood movies in the 1940s.

Warners had bought the story for this Arabic intriguer for $20,000 in 1941 after it had been rejected by several other studios. That, however, was not necessarily a bad sign in the movie business. What was less promising was that the story was based on a play that had never been produced because its authors had refused to make revisions—a sure sign, any editor will tell you, that something needed to be fixed. What writers think is the best stuff is very often the worst.

Could Bergman help fix this play's flaws? Wallis thought so, and he convinced Jack Warner, who ran the studio, to get Bergman. But Warner didn't think that was going to be easy. Not only was Selznick a pain in the neck to deal with—author and screenwriter Niven Busch, one of his boyhood friends, said Selznick acted like a jerk in those days after *Gone With the Wind*—but how do you sell a project to one of the toughest producers in Hollywood without a script, director, or cast?

You send writers, and Wallis and Warner had two of the best writers in Hollywood: Julius J. and Philip G. Epstein. The Epsteins were identical twins and two of the best screenwriters of their day, specializing in sophisticated urban comedy. Their forte was witty dialogue, which shows up in films like *Arsenic and Old Lace* (directed by Frank Capra and starring Cary Grant). After his brother died of cancer in 1951, Julius continued to be well-known and respected in Hollywood. In fact, he went on to write *Reuben, Reuben* and *House Calls*—two critical and financial hits in the 1970s and '80s, impressive efforts for a man then nearing seventy in an industry that has always lost interest in anyone with any hint of an age line.

In March 1942, the Epsteins met with Selznick and Bergman, but only after Selznick had been ducking Wallis for several weeks. Wallis, in fact, had to go to New York to ambush Selznick and convince him to discuss loaning Bergman. In his autobiography, Wallis describes learning that Selznick was staying at the Hotel Carlyle on Fifth Avenue across the street from Central Park. "I flew back, checked in there and called him on the house telephone," he said. "It paid off. He agreed to see me."

That must have been one of the great meetings in film history. Julius Epstein remembered that "Jack Warner . . . said we had to go to Selznick and talk him into letting us have Bergman and that David would want to know every detail of the screenplay. We said we didn't know what to say, but Warner told us to make up something, anything, just bring back Bergman. Phil and I were ushered into Selznick's office and I got things started by saying it was a romantic melodrama with a sinister atmosphere. Dark lighting and a lot of smoke. . . . Selznick slapped the desk top and said, 'That's all I need to know, you've got Bergman.'"

Bergman, meanwhile, was just as surprised. "Selznick said that he had confidence in [the Epsteins] and that they were coming over to tell us the story," Bergman told an interviewer in 1974. "And they came, and they were very vague about the story. They had an idea, but it was all, 'Maybe we'll do it this way,' and 'We'll probably do that,' and 'We're going to get a good cast.'"

To this day, it's still not clear what convinced Selznick to loan Bergman to Warner Bros. Jack Warner did agree to lend him Olivia de Havilland in exchange for Bergman, and that helped to seal the deal. But the most likely piece of the puzzle was falling into place—literally —in the Sierra Nevada mountains, 450 miles away from Los Angeles.

What Selznick had really wanted was for Bergman to star in Paramount's production of Ernest Hemingway's *For Whom the Bell Tolls*, the critically and popularly acclaimed novel of the Spanish Civil War. Bergman, figured Selznick, was perfect for Maria, the Basque peasant resistance fighter who falls in love with Gary Cooper's Robert Jordan. But Paramount, in its infinite wisdom, decided a ballerina named Vera Zorina was perfect for the role. This left Selznick with an unhappy Bergman under contract, but nothing for her to do. Wallis's timing was perfect. (Ironically, after shooting started on *For Whom the Bell Tolls*, Paramount's executives realized Zorina was a horrible mistake. She wasn't a great actress, but that wasn't the biggest problem. Most of the movie takes place in the mountains, and Zorina, a dancer, was terrified she was going to slip and fall and ruin her legs. Zorina was fired after shooting had started, and Bergman replaced her, earning her first Academy Award nomination.)

With the female lead in place, production did start to move along. Approximately six weeks later, on May 25, 1942, shooting began. There still wasn't an acceptable script, but the director, an autocratic Hungarian immigrant named Michael Curtiz, didn't let that bother him—not too much, anyway.

"From the very start, Hal Wallis was arguing with [the writers], and every lunchtime Mike Curtiz was arguing with Hal Wallis," Bergman remembered later. "There had to be all sorts of changes in the script. So every day we were shooting off the cuff: Every day they were handing out the dialogue, and we were trying to make some sense of it."

The script problems made everyone's job harder, from the most junior prop man to the director and stars. The male lead, a forty-three-year-old character actor named Humphrey Bogart (until then best known for his portrayals of the rival hood who always got killed by Edward G. Robinson in the final reel of many of Warners' gangster films), was furious with the delays and uncertainties. He was continually stomping off to his trailer in disgust.

Bogart, who was trained as a stage actor, always prided himself on his professionalism. When he came onto the set, he claimed, he was always ready, always knew his lines, and always hated to repeat a scene. And despite his reputation (which was apparently deserved) as a heavy drinker, he never showed up drunk or unable to work. Bogart's brand of professionalism, then, left him with little patience for the Hollywood way of doing things. (After he made *Sabrina* in 1954 with Audrey Hepburn, a friend asked Bogart what it was like to work with the twenty-five-year-old model and heartthrob. "OK," growled Bogart, "if you like to do the same scene thirty times.")

To make matters worse, Bogart's wife at the time, an ex-actress named Mayo Methot, was convinced Bogart and Bergman were having an affair. They weren't (Bogart wouldn't justify Methot's jealousy until 1944, when he fell for a nineteen-year-old Jewish model born Betty Perske, who would become a star as Lauren Bacall), but Methot would show up on the set ranting and raving anyway. This was typical of Bogart and Methot, who were known throughout Hollywood as "The Battling Bogarts." Every account of their seven-year marriage invariably includes the word "stormy."

AND DIRECTOR MICHAEL CURTIZ.

Bergman was intimidated by Bogart anyway, for he was seventeen years older than she was and was well known as a curmudgeon. She was so worried about working with him that she saw *The Maltese Falcon*, then Bogart's best-known picture, over and over before and during the filming of their movie. Meanwhile, Methot's fits, combined with the script problems, left Bergman completely baffled about how to react to Bogart's character. The writers (by this time, at least seven of them had worked on the picture) still didn't have a satisfactory script completed as shooting drew to a close at the end of July. Not only hadn't they decided how to resolve the love triangle involving Bergman, Bogart, and the character played by Paul Henreid, a Viennese actor who specialized in Eastern Europeans, but they were reportedly having trouble getting pages done in time for the day's shooting. Howard Koch, one of the writers, claimed in his memoirs that by the end of the movie, he was lucky to get the pages on the set by the morning the scene in the script was going to be shot.

"All the time I wanted to know who I was supposed to be in love with. . . ." Bergman said. "I didn't dare look at Humphrey Bogart with love because then I had to look at Paul Henreid with something that was not love."

Somehow, shooting ended on August 3. No one was happy with the finished product—the actors, the director, or the producer. Even Max Steiner, the composer who scored the soundtrack, was unhappy. The script contained several references to a song he considered a piece of popular drivel, something called "As Time Goes By." Steiner wanted to write an original song for the soundtrack to replace "As Time Goes By," which meant that several scenes would have to be reshot. That was fine with Wallis, who was unhappy with the reception accorded the movie's ending by a preview audience. They had found the ending, written by the Epstein brothers as they drove down Sunset Boulevard, unsatisfactory. Wallis was thinking about asking Curtiz to reshoot the ending, then redoing the scenes that contained the offending song. Wallis sent a memo to the studio's production manager on November 11, detailing the sets and props needed for the new ending, which apparently involved Bogart fleeing North Africa on a Free French freighter.

But it seems that destiny had a taken a hand. On November 8, several weeks after the preview audience's lukewarm reception, Anglo-

RICK: "SAM, FERRARI WANTS YOU TO WORK
FOR HIM AT THE BLUE PARROT."
SAM: "OH, I LIKE IT FINE HERE."

American forces invaded North Africa. This made the film topical, always an advantage. Bergman, meanwhile, was already shooting *For Whom the Bell Tolls*. Her hair had been cut extremely short for the role, and she looked nothing like her North African character. That all but eliminated reshooting the "As Time Goes By" scenes. Then, on November 12, Wallis received a telegram from Selznick, who had seen a preview of the film:

> "THINK IT IS A SWELL MOVIE AND AN ALL-AROUND FINE JOB
> OF PICTURE MAKING <STOP> TOLD JACK [L. WARNER] AS FORCI-
> BLY AS I COULD THAT IT WOULD BE A TERRIBLE MISTAKE TO CHANGE
> THE ENDING, AND ALSO I THOUGHT THE PICTURE OUGHT TO BE
> RUSHED OUT <STOP>"

And that's how *Casablanca* got made.

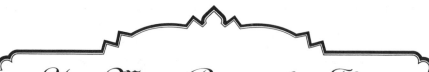

You Must Remember This

TRIVIA INTERLUDE #1

WHICH THREE OF THESE *CASABLANCA* STARS RECEIVED TOP BILLING?

Ingrid Bergman	Sidney Greenstreet
Peter Lorre	Conrad Veidt
Humphrey Bogart	Paul Henreid
Claude Rains	

Bergman, Bogart, and Henreid. It was one of the conditions of his contract that Henreid receive co-star billing.

HOW MANY MOVIES DID HUMPHREY BOGART AND INGRID BERGMAN MAKE TOGETHER?

Just *Casablanca*. Bogart's most frequent leading lady is Lauren Bacall, who starred opposite him in four films. He made more movies with Bette Davis (seven), and Ann Sheridan (six), but almost all of these came when Bogie was cast in a supporting role.

MATCH THESE CHARACTERS WITH THEIR *CASABLANCA* OCCUPATIONS:

1. Signor Ferrari	a. Prefect of police
2. Capt. Renault	b. Italian military attaché
3. Sacha	c. Piano player
4. Abdul	d. Cafe owner
5. Ugarte	e. Bartender
6. Carl	f. Doorman
7. Sam	g. Waiter
8. Capt. Tonelli	h. Black marketeer

Ferrari/cafe owner; Renault/prefect; Sacha/bartender; Adbul/doorman; Ugarte/black marketeer; Carl/waiter; Sam/piano player; Tonelli/military attaché.

HOW MUCH DID RENAULT BET RICK THAT VICTOR LAZLO WOULD NOT BE ABLE TO GET AN EXIT VISA TO LEAVE *CASABLANCA*?

10,000 francs (or, during the war, less than $1,000).

WHAT DID RICK DO TO EARN THE WRATH OF THE GESTAPO —TO DESERVE A SPOT ON THEIR "ROLL OF HONOR"?

He ran guns to the Ethiopians after their country was invaded by Italy in 1935 and fought for the government in the Spanish Civil War in 1936, when the Germans and Italians supported the Franco-led rebels. He was also involved in some sort of secret activities in Paris just before the city fell.

Who's Who in <u>*Casablanca*</u>

THE CREDITS

CREW

Producer: Hal B. Wallis
Director: Michael Curtiz
Writers: Julius J. Epstein &
Philip G. Epstein
and Howard Koch
Music: Max Steiner
Photography: Arthur Edeson
Film editor: Owen Marks

CAST

Rick Blaine: Humphrey Bogart
Ilsa Lund: Ingrid Bergman
Victor Laszlo: Paul Henreid
Captain Louis Renault: Claude Rains
Major Heinrich Strasser: Conrad Veidt

Ferrari: Sidney Greenstreet
Ugarte: Peter Lorre
Carl: S.Z. Sakall
Yvonne: Madeline LeBeau
Sam: Dooley Wilson
Annina Brandel: Joy Page
Berger: John Qualen
Sacha: Leonid Kinskey
Jan Brandel: Helmut Dantine
Pickpocket: Curt Bois
Emile the Croupier: Marcel Dalio
Singer: Corinna Mura
Mr. Leuchtag: Ludwig Stossel
Mrs. Leuchtag: Ilka Gruning
Captain Tonelli: Charles La Torre
Linen vendor: Frank Puglia
Abdul: Dan Seymour
Heinz: Richard Ryen
American: Monte Blue
French officer: Albert Morin
Gambler: Creighton Hale
German banker: Gregory Gay
Casselle: George Dee

Facts and Figures

Casablanca, despite being an "A" picture, was not particularly expensive to make. It cost $878,000—less than $100,000, or about eight percent, over budget. That wasn't cheap, but it wasn't a 1941 version of something like *Total Recall*, which cost $80 million in 1989. Perhaps more impressive is that the picture took just fifty-nine days to film, despite all of its script problems. Even more amazing is that those fifty-nine days were eleven over schedule. Imagine making a movie—even a made-for-TV movie—in six weeks these days.

Then compare those numbers to *Godfather III*, which took more than three times as long to film and cost fifty times as much to make.

One estimate is that *Godfather III* finished seven weeks behind schedule and was eleven percent over budget.

Casablanca also turned a profit (something *Godfather III* may not be able to claim), although it's almost impossible to tell how much. Hollywood didn't regularly release any sort of box office numbers until 1947, which makes any estimate of how much *Casablanca* grossed crude at best. Then there's the problem of trying to figure out how much the movie has made after its initial theatrical release from such things as video sales and rentals and television showings. The best guess, based on comparisons with similar films of the period, is that *Casablanca* garnered around $5 million for Warner Bros.—a 500-percent return on investment. That jibes with an estimate that *Variety*, the show business trade paper, made in 1990.

There were several reasons *Casablanca* was made so quickly and so inexpensively, and not all of them have to do with the rate of inflation between 1942 and 1992. The main one centers around the infamous studio system, which ruled Hollywood from the beginning of talkies until the late 1950s. Under the studio system, actors (along with directors and writers) signed a contract with one of the studios and could only work for the studio that held their contract. There were exceptions, of course; studios could and did lend actors to other studios in much the same way Selznick rented Bergman. But the underlying principle was that no actor worked unless his studio wanted him to work.

Eight studios were the linchpins of the system—the Big Five of MGM, Warners, Paramount, RKO, and Fox (later 20th Century-Fox) and the Little Three of Universal, United Artists, and Columbia. They made the pictures, distributed the pictures, and (in the case of the Big Five) owned the theaters that showed the pictures. It was, in economic terms, a classic example of a vertical monopoly. The studios paid themselves to make the pictures, paid themselves to distribute the pictures, and paid themselves to show the pictures. Even a poor businessman could have made piles of money with that arrangement. By the mid-1930s, nineteen of the twenty-five highest salaries in the country were paid to film executives. MGM boss Louis Mayer made more than $1 million a year even when the Depression was at its worst. Owning the theaters was the key to all of that money. One study estimates that the Big Five controlled almost three-quarters of the first-run theaters in the ninety-two largest cities in the country. In fact, the beginning of the

YVONNE: "WHERE WERE YOU LAST NIGHT?"

RICK: "THAT'S SO LONG AGO I DON'T REMEMBER."

end for the system came only after a federal antitrust action forced the Big Five to sell their theaters in 1949. This development paved the way for independent producers (who, often as not, were actors) and deprived the studios of a guaranteed market. The antitrust suit is still shaping the way films are made, even today.

Under the studio system, actors (save for a few notable exceptions) were unable to make a movie whenever they wanted to or with whomever they wanted to. They were bound to a studio for the length of their contract, usually seven years. If the studio said make a picture, they made a picture—one reason that Bogart, at the beginning of his career, made filler like *The Return of Dr. X*. They were paid by the week—often staggering sums for the period—but only when they worked. An actor under contract who turned down a role not only didn't get paid, but was placed "under suspension." Bacall, who became a star just as the studio system was collapsing, recalls tremendous fights with studio chiefs who wanted to cast her in movies she considered beneath her. Another crack in the studio system came in 1944, when Olivia de Havilland sued Warner Bros. to get out of her contract and won.

In the studio days, actors didn't get salaries such as the $10 million Sean Connery requires up front these days (even for a bad one like *Highlander 2: The Quickening*), and it was almost unheard of for actors to get a percentage of the picture's gross, which has become a standard practice in late twentieth-century Hollywood. Try to get Eddie Murphy to make a movie without giving him points—it's impossible.

Finally, there was almost no location shooting done on *Casablanca*. Every single scene but one—the initial airport sequence—was shot at Warners' Burbank studio. That accounts for the low cost— studio shooting is infinitely less expensive than location shooting—and for the cardboard look of many of the scenes. Where a director like Oliver Stone will travel the country for the correct milieu for a movie, studio system directors headed for the back lot.

Who Was Paid What

Casablanca was budgeted for eight weeks of shooting, and the following weekly figures are taken from that eight-week budget. In fact, most of the actors were paid more than was budgeted, since shooting went eleven days over budget. If these salaries seem like a lot of money today, imagine how much it seemed like then. Wrote producer Hal Wallis some forty years later: "We were dealing with actors being overpaid to sit around for weeks doing nothing because we weren't sure we would need them again."

♦ Bogart: $4,583
♦ Bergman: $3,125 (which Selznick got; Bergman received the $2,000-a-week salary her contract with Selznick called for)
♦ Henreid: $3,125
♦ Claude Rains: $4,000 (and he was freelance)
♦ Peter Lorre: $1,750 (and his contract, which was on loan to Universal, had to be bought out at $2,750 a week)
♦ Sidney Greenstreet: $3,750
♦ Conrad Veidt: $3,125 (not including $5,000 a week to borrow him from MGM)
♦ Dooley Wilson: $437.50 (which didn't include paying MGM, which was loaning him from Paramount, $3,500 a week)
♦ S.Z. Sakall: $1,750
♦ Leonid Kinskey: $400
♦ Joy Page: $200
♦ Michael Curtiz: $9,175
♦ Hal Wallis: $6,500
♦ Julius Epstein: $1,901
♦ Philip Epstein: $1,901
♦ Howard Koch: $525
♦ Secretaries: $793.75

Hum a Few Bars and I'll Try to Fake It

In 1931, a composer named Herman Hupfeld was commissioned to write songs for a Broadway revue called *Everybody's Welcome*. One of the songs he wrote was "As Time Goes By," which turned out to be a reasonably popular song in a reasonably popular show sung by the reasonably popular Frances Williams. And then the world forgot about the song.

Well, *almost* everyone forgot about the song.

Playwright Murray Burnett had always liked the song, almost wearing out a recording of it when he was a student at Cornell in the early 1930s. During a visit to a cafe called La Belle Aurore in the south of France several years later, he listened to a black piano player whose tunes reminded him of his college days. And his college days reminded him of "As Time Goes By."

Later, when Burnett and Joan Alison wrote a play about intrigue in North Africa called *Everybody Comes to Rick's*, he used "As Time Goes By" as the love theme for the male and female leads. Burnett had based the Rick's Cafe in the play on much of what he had seen at La Belle

RICK: "IF IT'S DECEMBER 1941 IN CASABLANCA, WHAT TIME IS IT IN NEW YORK?"

SAM: "WHAT? MY WATCH STOPPED."

Aurore, including the black piano player, so it seemed natural to incorporate the song into the play.

When the movie was completed, all of the writers (most of whom had lived in and around the New York area when the song was popular in the early 1930s) and Curtiz had left the song in. In all likelihood, they hadn't even noticed it; in most movies, the music isn't added until the initial filming is finished.

But Max Steiner, who wrote the score, did notice it—and he hated it. He told an interviewer in 1943, after the rest of the country was humming the tune to death, that he didn't think it was an appropriate love song for Bogart and Bergman. He was baffled by its success, even a year later.

Steiner's disregard for "As Time Goes By," insists one of the movie's scholars, had more to do with his desire to write an original song than any actual dislike of the song. If Steiner had written a love theme himself, he would have earned royalties every time it was played—and if the movie became any kind of a hit, that would add up to quite a piece of change.

Still, Steiner didn't let his personal preference interfere with his work. "As Time Goes By" is weaved expertly throughout the film, not only in the famous "Play It Again, Sam" scene (says Bogie: "You played it for her. You can play it for me. . . . If she can stand it, I can. Play it!" as the music roils in the background), but also when Bergman starts humming the song soon after entering the cafe. Talk about foreshadowing.

The Fundamental Things Apply
QUICK TAKES #1

◆ *Casablanca* was released on November 23, 1942, just fifteen days after the Allies landed in the cities of Algiers, Oran, and Casablanca in Operation Torch. Oddly enough, the invasion followed a chronology similar to that of the movie's production: Planning for the invasion began in April after several months of discussion, the decision to invade was made at the beginning of June, and the invasion was nine days behind schedule. The movie began preproduction work at the beginning of April, started shooting at the end of May, and finished eleven days behind schedule.

♦ *Casablanca* opened at the Hollywood Theater in New York City, eight months before its original release date of June 1943. Warners wanted to capitalize on the publicity surrounding the Torch landings. It played in selected big-city markets for the next six weeks, and then opened in the rest of the country in January 1943. That's why the film, which opened in 1942, won the 1943 Academy Award for Best Picture at the Oscar ceremonies in March 1944.

♦ *Casablanca* was one of the first twenty-five films selected for the National Film Registry in September 1989. The registry, established by Congress as part of 1988's National Film Preservation Act, honors films that are "culturally, historically or esthetically significant." Currently, there are seventy-five films on the registry. Joining *Casablanca* as inaugural honorees were such films as *Citizen Kane*, *Gone With the Wind*, *The Maltese Falcon*, and *Singin' in the Rain*.

♦ Humphrey Bogart looks so miserable in some of the early scenes in *Casablanca*, especially when he is playing a broken-hearted lover, because his love life was miserable. Bogart's marriage to Mayo Methot, never easy, was going through an especially difficult period. She called the studio frequently, threatening not only to come to the studio and disrupt filming but frequently promising to kill Bogart unless he broke off the affair she was convinced he was having with Ingrid Bergman. One of Bogart's biographers claims that she did try to kill herself, slitting her wrists ("but not very deep") shortly after filming ended.

♦ When Bogart meets Bergman in the market on the morning after his drunken denunciation of her unfaithfulness, he apologizes for his behavior. He blames it on the bourbon he was drinking, but doesn't pronounce it "burr-bun," the way everyone else does. Instead, he calls it "bore-bun," hardly the sort of mistake people would expect from such a famous boozer. But Bogart, who drank scotch, could have had another excuse: Bourbon was not particularly popular before World War II, and he was probably unfamiliar with it. Rye, which has almost died out in most parts of the country today, was the whiskey of choice for tough guys. The office bottle for Philip Marlowe, Raymond Chandler's archetypal hardboiled private eye, was rye.

♦ It's no coincidence that Bogart is playing chess when the camera sees him for the first time. Not only did chess figure prominently in one of the early versions of the script (Rick and Renault even get to trade some horrible dialogue about how "we're checkmated" in one proposed final scene), but Bogart was reportedly a first-class chess player. He, Claude Rains, and Paul Henreid would play during breaks in filming, and a publicity photo was taken of the trio consulting over a chess board.

♦ The letters of transit, which cause the death of four people and bring Victor Laszlo and Ilsa Lund to Casablanca, are (in most prints of the movie) signed by Charles de Gaulle. This was a change from the first "final" version of the film, when the letters were signed by Maxim Weygand, who commanded the Vichy French forces in Africa in 1941 (and who was the official who signed the letters in *Everybody Comes to Rick's*). The change was probably made for publicity reasons, for de Gaulle had, by the time the movie was released, become world-famous as the leader of Free France. The irony of the switch is that de Gaulle did not have any official standing in North Africa; in fact, he was a criminal, and would have been tried for treason if he had dared to set foot in Vichy-controlled territory. De Gaulle had as much authority to sign letters of transit "that cannot be rescinded, not even questioned" as an ordinary American does of ordering a nuclear strike.

The End

#1

The actor John Barrymore was famous for a variety of things: He was a member of one of the United States' most distinguished theatrical families (with brother Lionel and sister Ethel); he had been a matinee idol of some repute in the early days of sound; and he drank to excess. He drank so much, in fact, that it eventually killed him in 1942.

Since he drank so much, he was not an unfamiliar figure to Bogart and Peter Lorre, whose all-night binges were also common knowledge. "I try to drink only an ounce an hour, since I read that's all the liver could handle," Bogart once jokingly said of his drinking. Barrymore apparently had no such scruples. By the last year of his life, he had become a sad sight—an alcoholic who had alienated many of his colleagues and had worn out his welcome almost everywhere in Hollywood. One of his few remaining friends was Errol Flynn (like Bogart and Lorre, a Warners contract player). Barrymore spent much of the last months of his life at Flynn's home.

Toward the end of shooting on *Casablanca*, Barrymore died. That gave Lorre, who rarely passed up an opportunity for a practical joke, an idea. He and Bogart and Paul Henreid (who tells this story in his autobiography), along with several others, would bribe the funeral home director who had Barrymore's body to let the group use it to play a joke on Flynn.

"I know he's shooting and he gets home late," Lorre told the group. "We arrange [the body] in that chair in the living room he always used to sit in, and then we hide and watch Flynn's face. Is that or isn't it fantastic?"

Henreid writes that everyone was a little drunk when they discussed the idea, but that he wasn't so drunk that he didn't know discretion was the better part of valor. He backed out of the escapade, although he did contribute his share of the $200 bribe.

According to Lorre, Flynn entered the house, threw his hat and coat on a chair, walked across the room past the dead Barrymore, and headed for the bar. "He nodded at Barrymore and took about three steps, then froze. That moment was fantastic! There was a terrible silence, and then he said, 'Oh my God!' and he hurried back and touched Barrymore, then jumped. I think in that second he realized what was happening, and he shouted, 'All right, you bastards, come on out.'"

Flynn did offer to help the conspirators return the body.

• Two •
The Players

For the two generations raised on late-night television reruns, it's hard to believe that George Raft was one of Warner Bros.' biggest stars in the 1930s, and, in some quarters, the biggest attraction the studio had.

Anyone who remembers Raft for movies like *They Drive By Night* and *Background to Danger* will be shocked to discover that at the peak of his career, Raft may have been more popular than either James Cagney or Edward G. Robinson, the other two-thirds of Warners' three top male leads.

Cagney and Robinson, of course, started in gangster pictures and branched out to become respected actors. Cagney would display his dancing and singing skills in the musical *Yankee Doodle Dandy* (for which he won an Oscar) and as the spiteful ship's captain in *Mister Roberts*. Robinson went from playing stereotypical mobsters (*Little Caesar*) to roles almost as diverse as Cagney's. Anyone who thinks Robinson just made hoodlum pictures should see him in his final screen appearance in *Soylent Green*, where he acts rings around Charlton Heston.

That's a depth and a diversity that Raft never showed. After *Scarface* made him a star in 1932, he played the same part over and over and over—either a gangster with a heart of gold or one of those upstanding good guys of the 1930s and 1940s who always got Ann Sheridan at the end of the picture. There would be nothing like *White Heat*, where Cagney played a psychotic punk with a mother fixation, for Raft. One

BOGART, GEORGE RAFT, AND ANN

SHERIDAN IN *THEY DRIVE BY NIGHT.*

of the writers of *Background to Danger*, for example, complained to an interviewer that Raft forced the writers to change the lead character from a traveling salesman (an occupation that is important in the book the movie is based on) to an FBI agent. Raft, reported the writer, said he didn't want to play someone who sold typewriter ribbons.

Raft's refusal to take anything but comfortable parts is why he is no longer remembered with Cagney and Robinson. What he is remembered for, though, leads directly from that refusal: Raft played a key role in making Humphrey Bogart a star.

For Raft, in his determination to play nothing but good guys, enabled Bogart to get the two parts that helped him to cross the line from "B" pictures to "A"—and enabled him to show the skills that convinced Warners to cast him as Rick Blaine in *Casablanca*. That's a part, ironically, that Raft desperately wanted but never got.

Bogart's first break came in 1939, when Warners was casting a gangster picture called *High Sierra*. Producer Hal Wallis (who would produce *Casablanca*) wanted Raft to play "Mad Dog" Roy Earle, whose parole is arranged by a corrupt politician to pull one last job. But Raft, who didn't see Earle as a sympathetic enough character, refused. The part then went to Bogart, a long-suffering Warners contract player, more or less by default.

Bogart had been the studio's leading heavy since the middle 1930s, when he came to Hollywood from Broadway to play escaped killer Duke Mantee (a part he originated on the stage) in the Leslie Howard-Bette Davis film *The Petrified Forest*. For the rest of the decade, he either played the heavy who died in the final scene (eighteen in five years, in pictures like *The Roaring Twenties*, *Angels with Dirty Faces*, and *Kid Galahad*) or the lead in a host of "B" pictures so forgettable (typical are *Isle of Fury* and *Two Against the World*) that even Bogart would later be embarrassed to recall them. When he did get a different part, it was something as silly as the Irish horse trainer in 1939's *Dark Victory*. "Do you realize you're looking at an actor who made more lousy pictures than any other in history?" he asked writer Richard Gehman one afternoon. "I'm known as the guy who always squawks about roles, but never refuses to play one," he told another interviewer.

His battles with Warners to get better parts rarely did any good; instead, the studio would give him more money to shut him up (he was earning $75,000 a year in 1936, a considerable salary for someone who wasn't a star) and then assign him to a dog like *Men Are Such Fools* (directed by Busby Berkeley, of all people) to punish him for complaining. This was a common practice in the studio system days; Paul Henreid says RKO kept one particularly bad script around for just such purposes. When an actor got out of line and said he didn't want to play a certain part, he would then be offered this script, would refuse to do it, and would be suspended. Then, a studio executive would offer the actor the part he had originally balked at, and the actor, properly chastised, would take the original part.

The money was important to Bogart, who realized it was a sign of status in Hollywood—the more money you were paid, the more talented you were. This meant Raft, who was well-paid, was a huge talent (even though no one who writes about the period credits him with any acting ability at all). But the quality of Bogart's roles was important to him in a way that it wasn't to stars like Raft, who were more concerned with their public image.

This is because Bogart's first acting jobs were on the stage, where he became a well-known name in New York during the 1920s. Like many stage actors, Bogart was a snob when it came to his colleagues in the movies. This attitude would lead to trouble after he became a Hollywood star, when he had the clout to complain about working with former models and teen heartthrobs turned movie stars. But when he was only a contract player, he had few opportunities to vent his frustrations. "Why can't you be yourself, do your job, be your role at the studio and yourself at home and not have to belong to the glitter and glamor group?" he asked a gossip columnist in 1937. "I take my work seriously."

High Sierra doesn't seem to be any different from any other Warners gangster picture—a hood pulls a job, falls in love, is betrayed by a fellow hood, and gets shot by police in the final reel. But Bogart, director Raoul Walsh, and writers John Huston and W.R. Burnett (who would later tussle with Raft over *Background to Danger*) transformed it into something more. Earle is a metaphor not only for the passing of the Little Caesar-like gangster, but for the gangster picture as well (which Hollywood stopped making when World War II started and really never returned to).

The critical and popular acclaim for Bogart's performance in *High Sierra* stunned Warners executives. The studio heads, and Jack Warner

IDA LUPINO AND BOGART IN *HIGH SIERRA*.

in particular, had never thought of Bogart as anything more than a competent actor, and certainly not a romantic lead like Clark Gable or Cary Grant. But a review in the New York *Herald Tribune* said Bogart's performance made the movie more than just another Warners melodrama, and the crowds that greeted Bogart during a publicity appearance in New York were so large he was forced to move out of his hotel.

Then Raft lent Bogart another helping hand.

John Huston had been one of Hollywood's best writers in the 1930s, contributing not only to *High Sierra*, but to successes like *Jezebel* with Bette Davis and *Sergeant York* with Gary Cooper. Yet he wasn't satisfied with being just a writer; he also wanted to be a director. He had negotiated a clause in his contract with Warners that allowed

RICK: "HERE'S LOOKING AT YOU, KID."

him to direct one film; the studio had inserted it as a sop to his ambition. But Huston wanted to exercise the clause, and his choice was a novel by a private detective-turned-writer about a San Francisco private eye. Warners already owned the film rights to the book, and had made two versions of it (both of which flopped, including one with Bette Davis). Studio executives were less than thrilled with Huston's choice, but he pointed out that the movie, even if it failed, would both satisfy his contract and not cost too much to make.

But Huston wasn't planning on a failure. He would write the screenplay himself, using much of the novel's prose verbatim. He would also keep most of the characters and the atmosphere from the book, something neither of the previous versions had done. And he wouldn't have to worry about putting up with Raft.

In May 1941, Raft had been offered the part of Sam Spade, the movie's lead. Raft had just as quickly refused it. He wrote Jack Warner that his contract said he didn't have to make any "B" movies, and that he didn't consider this movie an "important" picture. Reportedly, he was also unhappy about working with an inexperienced director, acting in a remake, and playing a character as complicated as Spade, one of the screen's first anti-heroes.

Bogart was on suspension for refusing a part in a Western called *Bad Men of Missouri* (he was supposed to play outlaw Cole Younger) when Raft turned down the role of Sam Spade. Bogart had been the studio's second choice for the lead in Huston's movie, and he didn't hesitate on hearing the news: "Where the hell's the script, and when do I start?" A couple of days later, he started shooting his first starring role in an "A" picture.

So much for Raft's judgment. Huston's gem turned out to be Dashiell Hammett's *The Maltese Falcon*, and it is considered not only the finest mystery film ever made, but one of the best American films ever. It also made Bogart a star—maybe not of the Gable-Grant stature yet, but that would come within a year.

Bogart apparently never publicly acknowledged the continual boosts Raft gave his career (the latter also turned down a substantial part in *Dead End* that eventually went to Bogart). There is even a series of memos and letters from Bogart to Warners executives criticizing Raft for keeping him out of several films because Raft either wanted the parts or didn't want to play opposite Bogart.

Raft became, later in his career, even more famous for the parts he turned down than the parts he accepted: John Garfield got a juicy part in *The Sea Wolf* when Raft said no, and Fred MacMurray had a big hit with *Double Indemnity* after Raft bowed out. The list goes on.

But Raft would eventually realize what was happening. Said Raft, who had been born Georgie Ranft in New York's notorious Hell's Kitchen slum: "I didn't know much so I listened to guys who were supposed to know something."

For which movie fans throughout history will be eternally grateful.

PETER LORRE AND BOGART IN *THE MALTESE FALCON.*

You Must Remember This

TRIVIA INTERLUDE #2

WHAT'S IN A NAME? MATCH THE CHARACTERS WITH WHAT THEY CALL RICK BLAINE.

1. Mr. Richard
2. Ricky
3. Richard
4. Monsieur Blaine
5. Mr. Blaine
6. Rick
7. Herr Rick

a. Ugarte
b. Carl
c. Laszlo
d. Strasser
e. Sam
f. Ilsa
g. Renault

Mr. Richard/Sam; Ricky/Renault; Richard/Ilsa; Monsieur Blaine/Laszlo; Mr. Blaine/Strasser; Rick/Ugarte; Herr Rick/Carl.

WHO WAS INGRID BERGMAN'S MOST FREQUENT LEADING MAN?

Gary Cooper   Charles Boyer
Anthony Quinn   Cary Grant

Boyer. She made three films with him: *Gaslight* in 1944, *Arch of Triumph* in 1948, and the deservedly unknown *A Matter of Time* in 1976 (which was daughter Isabella Rossellini's film debut and the final film for Boyer and director Vincente Minnelli).

HOW MANY TIMES DID MICHAEL CURTIZ DIRECT HUMPHREY BOGART?

Six: *Kid Galahad, Angels with Dirty Faces, Virginia City, Passage to Marseille,* and *We're No Angels,* in addition to *Casablanca.* The most prolific Bogart director was Warners contract man Lloyd Bacon, who led him through seven films—mostly forgettable gangster flicks—between 1937 and 1943. The best was probably *Brother Orchid,* with

Edward G. Robinson as a mobster who hides out in a monastery after Bogart takes over his gang.

HOW MANY MOVIES DID BOGART MAKE WITH SIDNEY GREENSTREET?

Five. *The Maltese Falcon* (1941), *Across the Pacific, Casablanca, Passage to Marseille,* and *Conflict.*

BOGART IS ALMOST ALWAYS ASSOCIATED WITH PLAYING GANGSTERS OR PRIVATE EYES. YET HIS CHARACTERS SPANNED THE EMPLOYMENT SPECTRUM. MATCH THESE BOGART OCCUPATIONS WITH THEIR MOVIES:

1. Army doctor
2. Truck driver
3. Newspaper editor
4. Gun runner
5. Jet pilot
6. Gold prospector

a. *The Treasure of the Sierra Madre*
b. *Deadline USA*
c. *Chain Lightning*
d. *They Drive By Night*
e. *Sirocco*
f. *Battle Circus*

Army doctor/*Battle Circus*; truck driver/*They Drive By Night*; editor/*Deadline USA*; gun runner/*Sirocco*; jet pilot/*Chain Lightning*; gold prospector/*The Treasure of the Sierra Madre.*

BERGMAN, TOO, WAS TYPECAST, BUT IN THE GLAMOUR ROLES SHE PLAYED IN FILMS SUCH AS CASABLANCA AND INDISCREET. YET MANY OF HER PARTS WERE NOT GLAMOROUS. MATCH THESE OCCUPATIONS WITH THEIR MOVIES:

1. Receptionist
2. Governess
3. Trollop
4. Nun
5. Maid

a. *The Inn of the Sixth Happiness*
b. *The Bells of St. Mary's*
c. *Dr. Jekyll and Mr. Hyde*
d. *Adam Had Four Sons*
e. *Cactus Flower*

Receptionist/*Cactus Flower*; governess/*Adam Had Four Sons*; trollop/*Dr. Jekyll and Mr. Hyde*; nun/*The Bells of St. Mary's*; maid/*The Inn of the Sixth Happiness.*

Casting Casablanca

Hollywood is notorious for its casting faux pas. Sometimes, it seems to matter little if an actor is either talented enough for—or suited to—play a role. That's why it's not unusual to see an almost thirty-year-old Michael J. Fox acting like a teenager in the *Back to the Future* sequels. What's important, pointed out mystery novelist Robert Parker during a radio interview several years ago, is who's available. That's why stolid Robert Urich was miscast as Parker's private eye, Spenser—a sensitive fellow with a deep identity crisis about having to punch people out—in the television series of the same name.

That sort of reasoning was just as true fifty years ago, when Errol Flynn, the world's greatest swashbuckler, was forced to make a number of Westerns (including his turn as George Armstrong Custer in *They Died With Their Boots On*). And who can ever forget Jimmy Cagney in *The Oklahoma Kid*, where he shoots Humphrey Bogart in the last reel—both actors sporting chaps and six guns instead of fedoras and tommy guns?

In fact, it took a series of coincidences, several invisible nudges from the movie gods, and old-fashioned good luck to rescue *Casablanca* from the hands of the casting demons. Here's a look, part by part, at how the film came perilously close to starring Dennis Morgan, Ann Sheridan, and Ronald Reagan (as announced by *The Hollywood Reporter* in January 1942):

RICK BLAINE Besides George Raft, the studio considered either Morgan, a contract player who got the Cole Younger part in *Bad Men of Missouri* that Bogart had turned down, or Reagan. The sources (both original and secondary) aren't clear on whether Morgan was going to play Rick and Reagan was going to play Laszlo or vice versa. There's no doubt Raft wanted to play Rick, and there's no doubt that Wallis didn't want him. Hollywood legend says Raft turned down the part, but Wallis (even though he perpetuates the myth in his book) appears to have black-balled Raft despite Jack Warner's request to use him. Historian Rudy Behlmer has found a memo from Wallis to Warner dated April 2, 1942, rejecting Raft: "I have discussed this with Mike [Curtiz], and we both feel he should not be in the picture. . . . I don't think he should be able to put his finger on just what he wants to do when he wants to do it."

Morgan was a "B" leading man, one of dozens of what one film historian has called the pleasant young men who populated movies in the 1930s and 1940s. This made him as different from Bogart as possible, who was rarely pleasant and was especially difficult during the filming of *Casablanca* because of his failing marriage. The less said about Reagan the better (Ann Sheridan used to tell a story about dining with Reagan and then-wife Jane Wyman when Reagan recited all nine innings of a baseball game he had heard on the radio).

ILSA LUND Ann Sheridan spent most of her career playing America's Sweetheart (and eventually got so fed up with parts as kid sisters and best friends that she walked off the set of *The Strawberry Blonde* in 1943, giving Rita Hayworth her big break). She was as well-suited to play Ilsa as Reagan or Morgan was to play Rick. But to be fair, Sheridan was cast when the Ilsa character was called Lois Meredith, an American jet-setter. When the studio's writers changed Lois to Ilsa, Sheridan was discarded. Wallis wanted Bergman from then on, but David O. Selznick, who owned her contract, was balking. Warners tested a ballet dancer named Tamara Toumanova (the girlfriend of screenwriter Casey Robinson, who said he thought of making Ilsa a European so Toumanova could break into the movies); Wallis also asked MGM if he could borrow Hedy Lamarr, who had played a similar role in *Algiers*. Toumanova's test was apparently a failure, and Louis B. Mayer wasn't letting anyone use Lamarr. That left Bergman, and Selznick finally gave his permission.

VICTOR LASZLO Paul Henreid was almost not offered the part, since no one at Warners thought someone who claimed to be as serious an actor as Henreid did would take it. (Henreid, whose first contract included a clause to allow him time off to do theater, would later complain that no self-respecting resistance leader would go night-clubbing, let alone in a white suit.) But Philip Dorn, the studio's first choice, was filming *Random Harvest* and wasn't available. Then, tests were made of Carl Esmond and Jean-Pierre Aumont and found lacking, and Joseph Cotten was considered and unconsidered. Shortly after that, Wallis told director Michael Curtiz to resign himself to using someone like Dean Jagger (an American character player who looked, sounded, and acted like he was from Ohio—which he was). Henreid, however, finally relented. If Warners would give him co-billing with Bogart and Bergman and buy out part of his contract with RKO, he would take the role.

SAM Poor Dooley Wilson. After his screen test, Wallis told a colleague, "He isn't ideal for the part but if we get stuck and can't do any better I

Would You Believe...

RICK PLAYED BY . . .

RONALD REAGAN

GEORGE RAFT

VICTOR PLAYED BY . . .

DENNIS MORGAN

PHILIP DORN

ILSA PLAYED BY . . .

HEDY LAMARR

ANN SHERIDAN

SAM PLAYED BY . . .

LENA HORNE

suppose he could play it." And then Wallis considered what seemed like almost every black actor over thirty in Hollywood and New York—male and female. Among those Wallis looked at were Lena Horne, Ella Fitzgerald, a Manhattan society singer named Hazel Scott, and veteran character actor Clarence Muse (rejected, says Wallis, because his screen test was too much like a caricature of a black pianist). But on May 1, 1940, Wallis told Steve Trilling, the Warners casting chief, to sign Muse. Then he had a change of heart, and okayed Wilson. He would never be satisfied with Wilson's performance. Three weeks into shooting, Wallis wanted to hire someone to dub Wilson's singing voice, but was talked out of it.

Who's Who in Casablanca

THE CAST

HUMPHREY BOGART (born January 23, 1899, New York City; died January 14, 1957, Los Angeles) was one of the biggest stars in Hollywood in the 1940s, thanks to *Casablanca*. Before he died of cancer a decade later, he became one of the biggest stars in film history, a reputation that has not been tarnished thirty-five years later. It's almost impossible to over-estimate Bogart's influence on the movies—both in Hollywood and around the world—after he starred in *Casablanca*. He not only made the trench coat and fedora the uniform of the bitter, disaffected hero, but he made that bitter, disaffected hero a part of film lore. It's almost impossible to imagine the postwar film noir without the Bogart-type hero (see *Out of the Past* with Robert Mitchum), as well as the inevitable backlash (see Robert Altman's *The Long Goodbye* with Elliot Gould as the Bogart-like character). Even the French, film snobs of some repute, were fascinated by Bogart: François Truffaut's *Shoot the Piano Player* is the story of a lounge musician who wants nothing more than to wear a trench coat and talk out of the side of his mouth. Writer Raymond Chandler, who knew a thing or two about movie tough guys, said it best of Bogart: "All he has to do to dominate a scene is to enter it."

Bogart had struggled to achieve his success, which included three Oscar nominations and an Academy Award for *The African Queen*. He was thirty-seven before his role as Duke Mantee in *The Petrified Forest* established him as a film actor, and forty-two before he starred in his first "A" picture. This struggle didn't help Bogart's disposition, which

A PUBLICITY SHOT FOR *HIGH SIERRA*:
FEW ACTORS LOOKED AS NATURAL HOLDING A .45.

was never sunny to begin with. "The trouble with Bogart," said restaurateur Dave Chasen, "is that after eleven P.M., he thinks he's Bogart." Even his best friends knew better than to cross him when he was angry, and there are countless stories of his verbal bullying of those unfortunate enough—reporters, studio executives, other actors—to aggravate him.

His parents, a prominent upper West Side physician and a noted illustrator of children's books, were, according to several sources, not much happier, suffering through a miserable marriage. He had two

RICK: "NOTHING CAN STOP THEM NOW.
WEDNESDAY, THURSDAY AT THE LATEST THEY'LL BE HERE IN PARIS."

sisters, one of whom died as a child and another who had a nervous breakdown. He was married three times before he found a semblance of peace with Lauren Bacall after 1945 (yet there's a book by his former hairdresser who says she had an affair with Bogart before and during his last marriage). His first two marriages followed the same pattern (if not the extremes) of his seven years with Mayo Methot (nicknamed "Sluggy"), wife No. 3—a period of arguments and fighting followed by a brief reconciliation, followed by more fighting and more arguing. His relationship with his parents wasn't much better. His father, Dr. Belmont DeForest Bogart, died broke, leaving numerous debts. His mother, Maude Humphrey (from whom he got his first name), had been a noted magazine illustrator, and a baby Bogart had been one of her models. Still, she often told her son he would never amount to anything.

For years, it looked as if she would be correct. Bogart, kicked out of Andover Academy in 1918 for poor grades, spent two years in the U.S. Navy (where he may or may not have spent as much time in the brig as he did out of it—the story goes either way). After his discharge, he kicked around New York for six months, performing a variety of odd jobs. He eventually caught on as a stage manager for his parents' neighbor, theater producer William Brady. Bogart and Brady's son, Bill, had been childhood friends.

From there, it didn't require much nerve (and Bogart always had plenty of nerve) to try acting. His first role was the result of a dare from an actor who was tired of hearing Bogart whine about how easy actors had it. Bogart apparently had more nerve than skill in those early years; the noted critic Alexander Woolcott once said he was "what is usually and mercifully described as inadequate." Bogart never forgot the review, and his friends said he carried the clipping in his wallet until he died. It was not unusual for Bogart to pull the review out and show it to others. Between 1922 and 1934, he averaged more than a play a year, earning a reputation as a romantic juvenile. He worked with some of the leading actresses of the day—Judith Anderson, Ruth Gordon—in plays by renowned writers—Maxwell Anderson and Robert Sherwood. Bogart also spent two short stints in Hollywood, first with Fox in 1930 and then with Columbia in 1931, making nine movies that aren't even listed in most standard reference works.

His experience with Hollywood was so depressing that he returned to New York in 1931, promising never to leave Broadway again. He might not have if Sherwood, a friend of his, had not written a play about an escaped gangster, *The Petrified Forest*. Bogart met with Sherwood and the producer, Arthur Hopkins, to discuss a part in the play. "Hopkins said to me, 'I've got a good role for you. A gangster role,'" Bogart said years later. "Sherwood spoke up and said, 'Why you must be crazy. He doesn't fit that part at all!' . . . I thought Sherwood was right. I couldn't picture myself playing a gangster at all."

The role of the gangster—the stubble-faced Duke Mantee—changed his life. He was a smash on Broadway, where he starred with Leslie Howard. When Warners bought *The Petrified Forest*, they hired

Howard to recreate his role and wanted to cast Edward G. Robinson in the Bogart part. But Howard, who had become friends with Bogart during the play's six-month run (Bogart would name his second child Leslie after Howard), told Warners they couldn't have him if they didn't take Bogart. They took Bogart, who made a huge impression as Mantee. He never returned to Broadway.

That's because he never had the time. First, *The Petrified Forest* established him as a leading heavy, and then *Casablanca* made him one of the biggest stars of his era. Bogart signed a groundbreaking 15-year contract with Warners in 1947 that not only paid him $200,000 a year, but gave him casting, script, and directorial approval and allowed him to set up his own production company. Bogart's diverse roles after *Casablanca* showcased the skill that the gangster parts had only hinted at: as the paranoid Capt. Queeg in *The Caine Mutiny*; as the alcoholic screenwriter in *In a Lonely Place*; as the homburg-wearing businessman in *Sabrina*; and as the truly scary Fred C. Dobbs in *The Treasure of the Sierra Madre*.

INGRID BERGMAN (b. August 29, 1915, Stockholm; d. August 29, 1982, London) It's hard to believe that Bergman—who was as glamorous a star as the movies have ever seen—was a shy, lonely, and awkward child who was orphaned at the age of twelve.

But that is only one of the earliest contradictions Bergman poses. Her life, as Lawrence J. Quirk points out in his excellent essay in *The Films of Ingrid Bergman*, was a gigantic contradiction—"uncomplicated and well-adjusted on the surface, but who is in reality one of the most psychically labyrinthine and complex creative spirits ever. . . ."

It's probable that Bergman spent most of her life and career looking for the stability she never had as a child. How else to explain her three husbands, many affairs (reportedly with co-stars such as Spencer Tracy and Gary Cooper, and photographer Robert Capa), large family (four children conceived while she was working full-time as an actor in an era where women weren't supposed to work at all), and major careers in three places (Sweden, the United States, and Europe) and in three mediums (film, television, and the stage)?

But it would be unfair to reduce Bergman's life and career to some third-hand philosophizing. In many ways, she was one of the first women to successfully buck the studio system, both artistically and

ILSA: "IF YOU KNEW HOW MUCH I LOVE YOU,
HOW MUCH I STILL LOVE YOU. . . ."

personally. In 1946, after her seven-year contract with Selznick expired, she became a freelance actress, aligned with no studio. This was unusual enough, although her maverick career didn't produce any hits and included a dud with Alfred Hitchcock, *Under Capricorn*. But what really established Bergman as a woman who did what she wanted to do and Hollywood be damned was her 1951 marriage to Italian director Roberto Rossellini after a two-year affair that produced a son, Robertino, in 1950.

Hollywood was aghast. It was one thing to leave Selznick, who was paying her $2,000 a week for forty weeks a year while raking in six-figure payments for lending her to other studios ($150,000 from Paramount for *For Whom the Bell Tolls*). But to have a child by another man when she was still married to Dr. Peter Lindstrom—well, that was unacceptable to the residents of a city as straitlaced and puritanical as the movie capital of the world. The backlash, to say nothing of the hypocrisy, was so great she didn't make another movie in the United States for seven years.

Not that it bothered Bergman. "The press," she said a decade before her death, "kept insisting how unhappy I was in that period when actually I was very happy."

She made five movies with Rossellini during their seven-year marriage, and bore him three children. One of her daughters, Isabella, has since become a movie star, and it isn't hard to see where she got her exotic good looks. Bergman's movies in this period, however, weren't as fortunate. None were very good, for a variety of reasons. Rossellini worked without a script, and he liked to shoot in grainy black and white, facts that would have made his films difficult to distribute in this country even if there hadn't been a scandal surrounding the couple. The failures infuriated Rossellini and led to the breakup of their marriage. He was so macho, so Italian, Bergman said years later, that he couldn't stand his wife being a success when he wasn't.

Their marriage was annulled in 1958 (Rossellini had by then fathered a child by the wife of an Indian filmmaker; he was nothing if not consistent). Later that year, Bergman married a Swedish theatrical producer, Lars Schmidt. Her third husband, whom she divorced after seventeen years, arrived shortly after one of her greatest parts, the title role in *Anastasia*. It was the story of an amnesiac who may or may not be the long-lost daughter of the murdered czar of Russia, and earned Bergman the second of her three Academy Awards (she won a Best Supporting Actress Oscar in 1974's *Murder on the Orient Express*).

The irony of the part could not possibly have been lost on the woman who was orphaned as a child.

PAUL HENREID (b. January 10, 1908, Trieste, Austria-Hungary as Paul von Henried) made almost forty pictures between 1935 and 1984, yet only the most fanatical movie buff would be able to name two or three other than *Casablanca*.

This is a shame, because Henreid was not only a dashing and versatile actor (see his performances in swashbucklers like *Spanish Main* and *Thief of Damascus*, as well as his turn with Bette Davis in *Now, Voyager*), but a competent director (*Dead Ringer* and countless television programs, including some of the finest in Alfred Hitchcock's series).

Henreid, along with actors like Claude Rains, was ideal for the studio system. His versatility, Viennese accent (one critic has pointed out that in Hollywood in the 1930s and 1940s, one foreign accent was as good as another), and sophisticated good looks enabled him to star opposite women as diverse as Bergman, Davis, Maureen O'Hara, and Ida Lupino. It's no accident that his autobiography is called *Ladies' Man*—watch him light two cigarettes in his mouth, one for Davis and one for himself, in *Now, Voyager*.

Henreid was also a staunch progressive, as were many of the émigrés from fascism who flavored Hollywood in the years before and after World War II. He was one of the planeload of screen personalities (including John Huston, Gene Kelly, Lauren Bacall, and Bogart) who made the ill-fated trip to Washington to support the Hollywood Ten during the House Un-American Activities Committee hearings in 1947. The trip turned into a disaster; the ten writers under investigation for being Communists got into repeated shouting matches with committee members, losing whatever support they had in the country by sinking to the level of the mediocrities who made up HUAC. The trip even ended Henreid's friendship with Bogart, when the latter gave an interview afterward claiming he had been duped into supporting the Ten. In his book, Henreid says he was blacklisted by the studios for the next decade, which is why he gave up acting in favor of directing.

Henreid was in his late twenties when he was discovered working

LEFT: PAUL HENREID.
RIGHT: CLAUDE RAINS.

in the post-World War I Vienna theater by the influential German director Max Reinhardt (who also discovered one of Henreid's *Casablanca* co-stars, Conrad Veidt). He commuted between London and Vienna in the mid-1930s, and was in London when the Nazis annexed Austria in 1936. He did not return for four decades. After a successful career on the London stage and in British films (co-starring with Robert Donat and Greer Garson in *Goodbye, Mr. Chips*), he went to Hollywood in 1940. There, one of his first films was *Now, Voyager*, in which he played Davis's boyfriend. His work on the film, which was being shot while *Casablanca* was being cast, so impressed Hal Wallis that he all but begged Henreid to play Victor Laszlo.

CLAUDE RAINS (b. November 10, 1889, London; d. May 30, 1967, Sandwich, New Hampshire) There have undoubtedly been better actors in the history of the English-language cinema, but there have been few who did so many things as well as Rains did. He played an invisible man in his Hollywood debut, a princely usurper to the throne of England, a Nazi in love with Ingrid Bergman, a slimy U.S. senator who sees the error of his ways, a loving husband to Bette Davis, and a deformed composer who haunts a Paris opera house. And he was impeccable in almost every role.

His skills as a character actor were perfectly suited to the studio system. He was a short, middle-heavy, beady-looking man with an oily mustache, but those things—detriments to actors desperate to play leads—were advantages for someone who built a career playing parts that were slightly off-center. Rains enjoyed a latitude big stars didn't; how else to explain his undying popularity as the poor, corrupt prefect of police in *Casablanca*? In the role, he is not only the most beloved procuror in film history, but he comes perilously close to stealing the picture from Bogart. Not bad for an Englishman playing a Frenchman, is it?

Rains, between 1935 and 1950 (when, ironically, he was a freelancer), became the actor many of the studios counted on to round out the cast of their most prestigious "A" movies. This enabled him to work with some of the best directors of all time: Michael Curtiz (some half-dozen films, including *The Adventures of Robin Hood*), Alfred Hitchcock (*Notorious*), Frank Capra (*Mr. Smith Goes to Washington*), Mervyn LeRoy (*Anthony Adverse*), and David Lean (*Lawrence of Arabia*). About the only sort of film Rains never made was the Western; otherwise, his career included romances, thrillers, and swashbucklers. He was nominated for four Academy Awards between 1939 and 1946 (although he didn't win, losing to such luminaries as Charles Coburn). He was also a versatile husband, marrying five times.

Rains began his career at eleven on the London stage, then came to the United States before the start of World War I. He starred in the New York theater in the 1920s, working with the prestigious Theatre Guild. He went to Hollywood in the early 1930s, and was a hit in his first film, *The Invisible Man* in 1933. Even more remarkable was the critical praise for a part in which he was visible only briefly. (The part *was* a perfect showcase for his throaty, expressive voice.) After making a string of pictures that elicited little interest in the next five years, he signed to play Prince John in Warner Bros.' *The Adventures of Robin*

Hood. He was memorable in a part with few scenes, standing out despite the presence of Errol Flynn, Basil Rathbone, and Olivia de Havilland. His first Oscar nomination, for Best Supporting Actor in Capra's *Mr. Smith Goes to Washington,* followed a year later.

PETER LORRE (b. June 26, 1904, Rozsahegy, Hungary, as Ladislav Loewenstein; d. March 23, 1964, Los Angeles) was already a respected member of the Hollywood character actors fraternity when John Huston cast a little-known sixty-one-year-old named SIDNEY GREENSTREET (b. December 27, 1879, Sandwich, England; d. January 19, 1954, Los Angeles) in *The Maltese Falcon* in 1941. The two men would be linked forever afterward.

Between 1941 and 1946, the pair made nine films together, usually in supporting roles that to this day define Hollywood's idea of foreign intrigue. Greenstreet came to personify the blustering, scheming European who would entrap the innocent American (even when played by Bogart) at every opportunity; Lorre would offer an even darker, more sexually perverse view of the Old World. Many of their films together remain classics of the studio system, *Casablanca* and *The Maltese Falcon* among them. But the duo were also memorable in lesser-known films such as *Three Strangers* (where they played two-thirds of a troika that holds a winning lottery ticket) and *The Mask of Dimitrios* (where Lorre got to play the lead).

Lorre's strength was his ability to use his weasel-like looks to insinuate himself with an audience. In *Casablanca,* for instance, he is shot and killed after just two scenes, yet his performance ("What right do I have to think?" he asks Rick) has become so engrained in film tradition that it has become almost a stereotype. In fact, Lorre became an international star after playing the child molester in Fritz Lang's *M* in 1931 (a performance one leading reference work cites as one of the greatest in the history of the cinema), and many of his roles in the next thirty years were variations on that theme.

But his versatility, like Rains's, was legendary. His role in the eight *Mr. Moto* films between 1937 and 1939 helped turn what could have been silly, crude, B-grade efforts into something that is still watchable today. That's a neat trick for an Austrian playing a Japanese detective in the era of the Yellow Peril. Lorre was also a standout in comedy (*Arsenic and Old Lace*) and musicals (*Silk Stockings*).

GREENSTREET AND LORRE WITH GERALDINE FITZGERALD IN *THREE STRANGERS*.

Greenstreet's impact on Hollywood was more immediate (and was as large as his 285-pound girth). He had been a respected stage actor for almost forty years, and was touring with Alfred Lunt and Lynn Fontanne when Huston saw him in a play in Los Angeles. The writer-director was so impressed that he asked Greenstreet, who had vowed never to make a movie, to take the part in *The Maltese Falcon*. An Academy Award nomination for Best Supporting Actor followed. Even more amazing is that Greenstreet specialized in comedy on the stage, usually playing droll butlers; yet many of the twenty-four roles in his nine-year film career were of arch-villains dedicated to the destruction of the American way of life. Typical was *Across the Pacific*, in which he tried to sabotage the Panama Canal for the Japanese. Still, he retained a flair for comedy, as anyone who has seen him as the priggish magazine editor in the otherwise sappy *Christmas in Connecticut* can testify.

In May of 1943, Warner Bros. announced an upcoming movie entitled *The Conspirators* that would "re-unite the male members of the cast of *Casablanca*"—specifically, Bogart and Henreid. The movie, re-

HEDY LAMARR WITH MEMBERS OF THE WARNERS

STOCK COMPANY IN *THE CONSPIRATORS.*

leased a year later without Bogart, strove for the first film's atmosphere, but with only middling results. (Even *Casablanca*'s stylish banter was attempted, albeit unsuccessfully: "How long will you be staying?" "Not long." "What a pity. Where will you be going?" "Away.") Henreid plays a suave guerrilla leader from Holland who falls in love with a mysterious beauty played by Hedy Lamarr. Set in Lisbon and directed by the dependable Jean Negulesco, the film is sporadically entertaining, thanks in large part to the veteran supporting cast headed by two other *Casablanca* alumni—Sidney Greenstreet and Peter Lorre.

CONRAD VEIDT (b. Hans Walter Konrad Veidt, January 22, 1893, Potsdam, Germany; died April 3, 1943, Los Angeles) By the time Veidt was cast in *Casablanca*, he had been acting for more than two decades. In fact, he was so well-known to his peers and to audiences that MGM demanded $5,000 a week to loan him to Warner Bros. to play Major Strasser. This was twice as much as the studio was paying to borrow Ingrid Bergman.

This will no doubt come as a surprise to modern filmgoers, who might know Veidt's face but who would have a hard time remembering him by name. And if they know Veidt at all, it is only as the sneering, thin-lipped Nazi who cross-examines Humphrey Bogart while eating caviar.

But Veidt had established a reputation for excellence in the film industries of two other countries long before his character matched wits with Bogart's Rick Blaine. He was memorable as the magician Jaffar in the classic 1940 British production, *Thief of Baghdad*, and he played a sleepwalking killer in the landmark German Expressionist film, *The Cabinet of Dr. Caligari*, in 1919. He made just eight films in Hollywood, all in the final three years of his life after leaving wartime Britain.

Veidt's career began before World War I, when he studied with the legendary impresario Max Reinhardt (who also discovered Paul Henreid) in Berlin. He then served in the German army before being discharged with jaundice. This turned out to be the opportunity his film career needed. Since most of the country's actors had been drafted, the stage-trained Veidt was constantly in demand. His first film was the 1917 German production, *Der Spion* (*The Spy*).

Veidt would play countless numbers of German spies and officers throughout his career (including a turn in the 1942 *Nazi Agent* as both

CONRAD VEIDT.

an evil spy and the spy's good-guy twin brother). There are a number of ironies to this, not the least of which is that Veidt was typecast as a Nazi villain even though he had fled the Hitler regime. Veidt, who had never agreed with the Nazi Party's politics, was also married to a half-Jewish woman. He emigrated to Britain in the early 1930s, despite Nazi attempts to convince him to stay. No less a personage than Propaganda Minister Joseph Goebbels guaranteed his and his wife's safety, for Veidt was that big a star in the German cinema.

MICHAEL CURTIZ (b. December 24, 1888, Budapest, Hungary, as Mihaly Kertesz; d. April 10, 1962, Los Angeles) History has not been kind to Curtiz, the best director Warner Bros. had during its heyday in the 1930s and 1940s. His hits—both critically and at the box office—are among the best in the history of the American cinema. Are there better swashbucklers than *The Adventures of Robin Hood* or *The Sea Hawk*? How many musicals are better than *Yankee Doodle Dandy*? Which gangster pictures surpass *Angels with Dirty Faces*? And just try to ignore *Casablanca*.

Yet when the great American directors are mentioned, Curtiz is ignored. In his influential 1968 book, *The American Cinema*, film critic and scholar Andrew Sarris relegated Curtiz to the sixth of his ten tiers of directorial excellence. "If many of the early Curtiz films are hardly worth remembering, none of the later ones are even worth seeing," he wrote, and consigned Curtiz to oblivion with directors like Delmer Daves, who made *Demetrius and the Gladiators*. Richard Schickel wasn't much kinder in his *The Men Who Made the Movies* in 1975; he writes about Hitchcock, Capra, Hawks, John Ford, Raoul Walsh, George Cukor, Vincente Minnelli, King Vidor, and William Wellman— but not Curtiz. Curtiz receives only passing mention in the standard *An Introduction to American Movies*, where *Casablanca* is shrugged off as a "minor classic," and where Hawks, Ford, and Hitchcock are given as examples of the French *auteur*. Meanwhile, the well-known critic Pauline Kael once dismissed Curtiz's technique as "simple."

What's wrong with these people? "He was, in my opinion, one of the best we've ever had and is still much underrated in these days of auteur preoccupation," said Vincent Sherman, a director who worked with Curtiz at Warners.

That's also the theory behind Barry Paris's article in *American Film* in December 1990, where he points out that Curtiz may have been so good that he was taken for granted. He did what he was told by the studio moguls, and he almost always did it well. Warners, for instance, depended so heavily on Curtiz that he made eighty-eight films for the studio between 1926 and 1954, and it wasn't unusual for him to direct four or five pictures a year in the 1930s. When *Robin Hood*'s original director, William Keighley, was fired with the movie over budget, behind schedule, and missing the point, the studio simply inserted Curtiz. Reported the unit manager: The film "was moving along 100% better." The director was nominated four times for Oscars (but won only once, for *Casablanca*).

Of course, Curtiz never pretended to be a genius. He never

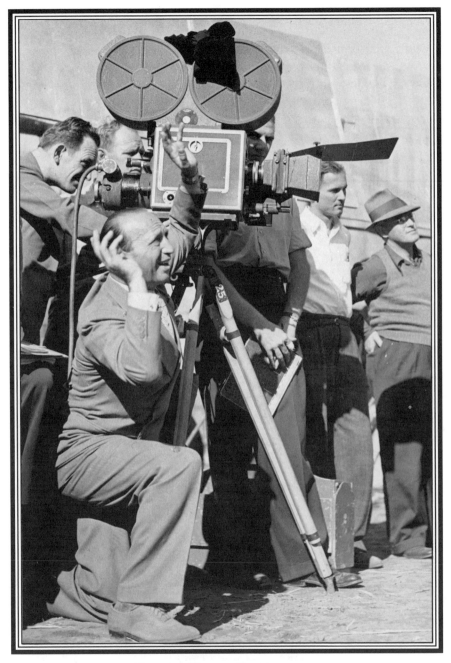

DIRECTOR MICHAEL CURTIZ AT WORK.

boasted he could make a good movie out of Hemingway's worst book, as Hawks did of *To Have and Have Not*. He made few movies on location, so the accolades that went to Ford for discovering Monument Valley would not be his. He never devised a theory of filmmaking like Hitchcock's "MacGuffin," thus leaving little for the critics to talk about. What he had was the ability learned in silent films to keep the camera moving (Paris insists that it was Curtiz's always-active camera, and not Flynn's athletic ability, that made Flynn the greatest swashbuckler ever) and to use lighting effectively. Curtiz isn't listed as one of the pioneers of film noir, but anyone who has seen the shadows in *Casablanca* and *Mildred Pierce* knows better. Those are techniques Curtiz learned when he was working with the German Expressionists in the 1920s.

Curtiz never pretended to be a Hollywood swell fellow, either. His English was miserable, and his malapropisms, though less famous than mogul Sam Goldwyn's, were funnier. David Niven called his auto-biography *Bring On the Empty Horses* in honor of Curtiz's command to let loose a herd of riderless horses during the filming of *The Charge of the Light Brigade*. Perhaps the best was his denunciation of a crew member who failed to bring the correct prop to the set: "Next time I send a damn fool, I go myself."

But these sort of goofs were to be expected of a Hungarian immigrant who spent the first decade of his professional life making some of Europe's earliest blockbusters. They included the most expensive Austrian film made up to that time, what is considered the first Hungarian movie ever made, and the German *Moon of Israel* in 1926, which attracted Harry Warner's attention. There are almost as many stories of his birth and childhood—to a noble family, to an architect, to a lowly carpenter—as there are films to his credit. The story of his later life—cavalry officer, artillery gunner, circus strongman, Olympic fencer—isn't much clearer.

What is clear is that he was tyrannical on the set as well as a noted womanizer. His feuds—with Bette Davis among others—were legendary. Curtiz made Flynn a star in *Captain Blood* and directed him in ten other films, but they couldn't stand each other. Curtiz called him "Erl Flint" to annoy the actor and, Flynn insisted in his autobiography, forced the actors to use swords without safety points during the climax of *Captain Blood*. Flynn, for his part, continually mocked Curtiz's English and forced the director off *They Died With Their Boots On* by refusing to work with him. Ironically, Flynn had few hits, either commercial or critical, after that 1941 episode.

The Fundamental Things Apply

QUICK TAKES #2

◆ Don Siegel, who would become one of Hollywood's most popular and critically acclaimed directors in the 1960s and 1970s (*Dirty Harry, Invasion of the Body Snatchers*), got his start at Warners in the film library in the 1930s. He later became head of the montage department, editing those oft-used scenes that display the passage of time, such as pages falling off a calendar. Anyone looking for an influence in Siegel's career need look no further than his association with Curtiz; Siegel did the montages on a number of Curtiz films, including *Casablanca, Yankee Doodle Dandy*, and *Passage to Marseille*.

◆ *Casablanca*, a movie about refugees from Nazi persecution, features a number of refugees from the Nazis. Henreid, Lorre, even Conrad Veidt, who played Gestapo Major Strasser, were among the actors who fled Hitler's Germany in the years before World War II. But none of them knew what it was like to be a refugee as well as Madeline LeBeau (Yvonne) did. She had managed to escape from occupied France just months before filming began. It didn't take much acting for her to cry during the Marseillaise scene.

◆ Dooley Wilson, despite Hal Wallis's objections, was an accomplished singer. What he couldn't do was play the piano. During the filming of *Casablanca*, a Warners staff musician, Elliott Carpenter, played the piano to the side of the set so that Wilson could get his bearings. It's also Carpenter's playing that was dubbed into the film. The charade went off so well that when Wilson appeared for a nightclub gig after the movie was released, the club's manager asked him why he wasn't going to play the piano in his act.

◆ Curtiz went freelance after leaving Warner Bros. in 1954, and his films ranged from Elvis Presley's *Kid Creole* (the only Elvis film to meet with any kind of critical success) to his final film, the John Wayne Western, *The Comancheros*. But his most interesting assignment came the year he left Warners, when he directed Bing Crosby and Danny Kaye in *White Christmas*. The movie, which used some songs from another der Bingle musical *Holiday Inn*, has its highlights, but the attraction for Curtiz fans is the director's motivation: He needed money to pay for a lawsuit brought by a twenty-two-year-old woman who claimed Curtiz, sixty-six, was the father of her illegitimate baby.

◆ Humphrey Bogart liked to drink, but he didn't like to eat. After he became a star, he would spend long afternoons at Romanoff's, the in restaurant in Hollywood, where he had the best booth. His lunch would be nothing more than bacon, eggs, and coffee, preceded by martinis and followed by Drambuie. He brought his young son Steven once, and after the fifth drink, Steven was ready to go home. Bogart was just getting started.

◆ Curtiz didn't want to direct *Casablanca*. He told Wallis, who was one of his few close friends in Hollywood, that he didn't feel comfortable directing that sort of picture (although Wallis doesn't say what "that sort of picture" is). But that was okay with Wallis, because Curtiz wasn't his first choice. William Wyler (*The Best Years of Our Lives* and *Ben-Hur* among countless others) was, and Wallis tried to contact him. But Wyler never returned Wallis's call. He was, several sources insist, playing high-stakes gin rummy with 20th Century-Fox mogul Darryl Zanuck and couldn't be bothered.

◆ Considering that David Selznick sold Ingrid Bergman on *Casablanca* by telling her she could wear a lot of pretty dresses, it's revealing to note that her wardrobe was not especially glamorous. Bergman wears a couple of practical hats, three or four sensible suits, and a jumper that just as easily could have been worn in Florida as in French Morocco. Even when she makes her dramatic entrance after Ugarte is shot, Bergman is wearing nothing more than a well-tailored white suit. "Every dress I wear in *Casablanca*, I could wear today," she said in 1974, and despite fashion's never-ending changes, this statement is just as true in 1992. Producer Hal Wallis was responsible for much of this continuity; he realized (as he wrote in memos to the production staff and to costume designer Orry-Kelly) that the wife of a resistance leader would not run around in fancy ball gowns, no matter what the precedent in Hollywood had been.

The End

#2

Hal Wallis was one of the most respected producers in Hollywood from 1930 until the early 1970s. He started with *Little Caesar* and was still a respected and powerful executive when his *Anne of a Thousand Days*

PRODUCER HAL WALLIS.

was nominated for the Best Picture Oscar in 1970 when he was seventy-one. Along the way, he produced everything from Elvis Presley movies to Charlton Heston's first starring film (*Dark City*) to John Wayne Westerns (*The Sons of Katie Elder*) to literate costumers (*Becket*). Under his

63

leadership between 1933 and 1944, Warner Bros. made a fortune and earned a critical reputation with pictures ranging from *Casablanca* to *The Life of Emile Zola* (a good example of the bio-pics that made Paul Muni a star).

But that success didn't seem to make any difference to Jack Warner, whose disagreements with Wallis turned into a feud that lasted until each man died. In 1965, when Warner wrote his autobiography, he mentioned *Casablanca* only to compare it to *Pride of the Marines*; he mentioned Wallis only once, and that was to imply he was stupid.

Wallis started with Warners in 1922 as an assistant in the publicity department. Six years later, he had worked his way up to head of production, only to be displaced by Darryl Zanuck in 1931. Zanuck lasted just two years with the Warners, who were notoriously difficult to work with—even in a city like Hollywood, where everyone was difficult to work with. Brothers Jack and Harry Warner, for instance, didn't speak to each other for twenty years.

After Zanuck's departure, Wallis was once again named head of production. This made him the third-most powerful man on the lot after studio chief Jack Warner. (Harry Warner, the most powerful, was the company president, Samuel Warner had died in 1927, and Albert Warner worked in New York handling distribution.) His role at Warners made Wallis one of the half dozen most influential men in Hollywood, on a par with legendary moguls like Louis Mayer at MGM.

One of the keys to Wallis's success was the personal interest he took in each of the films the studio produced. There are production notes in the Warner Bros. archives at USC for a number of Wallis-produced pictures, and they show the meticulous attention he gave each film. He discusses everything from individual camera shots to specific music for specific scenes. In *Casablanca*, for instance, he told Max Steiner to use "Perfidia" in the score. This attention to detail twice helped Wallis earn Irving Thalberg awards from the academy for excellence in making pictures while he was at Warners, and three Oscar nominations after he left.

Casablanca is one of the pictures for which many of Wallis's notes still exist, and they show a man driven to make the movie a critical and popular hit (his feelings about Dooley Wilson notwithstanding). He took an especially active role in fixing the script and in editing the picture after shooting was completed. He is also credited with helping to devise the final airport scene. Among the producer's other contributions: Henreid, as Laszlo, was going to wear evening clothes instead of his white suit until Wallis intervened; and he constantly intervened between Bogart and Curtiz during shooting, for they argued often.

That's why, when *Casablanca* won its Academy Award for Best Picture, Wallis got up from his seat and started to make his way to the stage to accept the award. It was the custom then, as it is now, for the producer, not the studio executive, to accept the Best Picture Oscar.

That's "when Jack [Warner] ran to the stage ahead of me and took the award with a broad, flashing smile and a look of great satisfaction," Wallis wrote in his 1980 autobiography. "I couldn't believe it was happening. *Casablanca* had been my creation; Jack had absolutely nothing to do with it. As the audience gasped, I tried to get out of the row of seats and into the aisle, but the entire Warner family sat blocking me. I had no alternative but to sit down again, humiliated and furious. Almost forty years later, I still haven't recovered from the shock."

Wallis's contract did not expire for two more years; when it did, he left Warners to become an independent producer. He never worked with Warners again.

◆ *Three* ◆
Who Wrote
Casablanca?

*I*f there was ever a period in the history of the printed word when being a writer was actually as glamorous as it is made out to be, it was in Hollywood in the 1930s and 1940s, at the height of the studio system.

The eight major studios employed more than one thousand writers, probably the largest conglomeration of literary talent ever assembled. The roster was a who's who of American fiction in the twentieth century—detective writers like Raymond Chandler and Dashiell Hammett, bon vivants like Dorothy Parker and S.J. Perelman, and a staggering number (such as Nathanael West and Aldous Huxley) who are still required reading in high school English classes. Even the heavyweights, the writers who changed American fiction like William Faulkner and F. Scott Fitzgerald, eventually made their way to Hollywood. (What happened to them there is another story.)

Hollywood offered the writers security, prestige, and tremendous amounts of money (to say nothing of booze and women, if the stories are to be believed). This was probably the only time the average writer was paid more than the average baseball player. A junior writer, generally a young man who had published a short story somewhere and displayed a touch of talent, started at $75 a week—not bad money in the late 1930s, when coffee cost a nickel a cup and a meal in a good restaurant went for less than a dollar. Plus he got an office, a secretary, and a seat in the studio commissary.

And the studios, in their desperation for scripts (the eight majors totaled more than five hundred films a year), could be much more appreciative. Nunnally Johnson (*The Grapes of Wrath, The Dirty Dozen*) was fairly typical of the "A" screenwriters during the studio system years. He started as a junior writer in 1932 at $300 a week after a moderately successful decade as a newspaperman and contributor to *The Saturday Evening Post*. To put that $300 a week into perspective, remember that the Depression was under way and that twelve million people were unemployed—probably one third of the work force. And know that even today, there are beginning newspaper reporters with college degrees who are lucky to get $300 a week.

When a writer hit it big, the money was obscene. Ben Hecht, generally regarded as the best screenwriter of the period, received $15,000 in 1939 for a week's work doctoring the script for *Gone With the Wind* (which, in 1992 currency, is probably close to a quarter of a million dollars). Chandler, who for all of his whining and moaning was one of the most successful (and best-paid) screenwriters of the 1940s, signed a contract in 1946 that paid him $4,000 a week—enough to buy four new luxury cars a week. Hammett, far less successful as a screenwriter, was paid $40,000 for a treatment of the third *Thin Man* movie in 1937.

Of course, the writers didn't think they were getting such a good deal. One of the legends that shows up in every account of Hollywood during that period tells of the writer (a variety are mentioned, including *Casablanca*'s Epstein twins) who was required to clock in every day at nine A.M. This, of course, wreaked havoc on anyone who had been up all night with his blondes and booze. "I'm a creative man, an artist," the writer supposedly tells the heartless studio mogul. "I can't work under the tyranny of the time clock. I must work my own hours, at home!" Then, after the mogul turns him down, the writer submits a crummy script. When the mogul demands to know why the script is so bad, the writer feigns ignorance and strikes a blow for the *artiste* everywhere: "How can it be bad? It was written at the office at nine A.M.!"

To be fair, it wasn't all blondes and bourbon during those two decades. Writers worked under contracts whose length and option were determined by the studio. If at the end of a typical six-week contract some producer didn't like a writer's work (or his personality), the producer fired him. Week-to-week contracts weren't unusual, and

ILSA: "WITH THE WHOLE WORLD CRUMBLING

WE PICK THIS TIME TO FALL IN LOVE."

ninety percent of the writers, by one estimate, made less than $10,000 in 1934. The hours and deadline pressures, too, didn't seem to leave much time for fooling around: Nathanael West tells of writing two scripts in seven weeks, working six days a week.

But what really galled the writers—a tremendous number of whom were literate, articulate, and well-read college graduates—was working in a system run by little-educated moguls whose native language often wasn't English and who seemed to consider their writers as "schmucks with Underwoods." Writers were not allowed on the set during filming, were not invited to premieres, and were not guaranteed screen credit. Instead, they spent their time writing, rewriting, and re-rewriting; it was a perfectly ordinary process when two writers collaborated on a script, and then two, three, or four other writers would revise it, one after the other. Some writers specialized in snappy dialogue, while others handled love scenes or action scenes. Still others wrote for specific stars.

Typical was what happened to the screenplay for *Yankee Doodle Dandy*, the musical about George M. Cohan that earned Jimmy Cagney an Oscar. The screen credit went to Robert Buckner and Edmund Joseph; in fact, Julius and Philip Epstein wrote much of the film, revising the scripts written by Joseph and then Buckner. This, Julius Epstein said, was so common as to be hardly worth mentioning, and no one found out about it for forty years. "Everybody at the studio was a script doctor," he told an interviewer in 1983. "[It was] 'Who isn't doing anything at the moment? Here, see what you can do with these scripts.'"

Given all of this, it's hard to believe that one of the biggest controversies in Hollywood history revolves around the *Casablanca* script. In many ways, it's no different from any other movie of the studio system, where the script was almost always written by committee. Yet that, perhaps, is one of the best reasons why *Casablanca* is more than just another movie. Very few books, let alone doctoral dissertations, have been written about the script for *The Song of Bernadette*, which was also nominated for a Best Picture Oscar in 1943. But it's easy to figure out why. No one in *The Song of Bernadette* gets to say, "Of all the gin joints in all the towns all over the world, she walks into mine." There are no wild tales of frantic writers penning pages, barely finishing in time to avoid a shutdown on the set.

It is, after all, a little mind-boggling that a film as tightly written and constructed as *Casablanca*, and which doesn't have any wasted scenes, could have been put together on the spur of the moment, as *Casablanca* supposedly was.

Yet reputations have been made, and friendships have been lost, in trying to determine who wrote how much and when they did it. One critic, Harry Haun, went so far as to break the script down line by line to learn its secrets. Warner Bros. contract writers Julius J. and Philip G. Epstein shared the Oscar for Best Adaptation with their colleague Howard Koch, but that doesn't even begin to solve the controversy. It's almost impossible to use the screen credit as a road map, for Screen Writers Guild rules in 1941 called for only two writers of writing teams to receive credit. A dissatisfied writer could have taken the matter to Guild arbitration (which none of the claimants did), but only to become one of the two listed on the screen. And although there is a wealth of first-hand information about the making of the movie in the form of autobiographies and interviews, many accounts conflict and the rec-ollections of dates and time sequences are often vague (as befitting the memories of men and women in their seventies and eighties recalling something that had happened thirty, forty, or fifty years before).

Koch, in his two books about the movie, takes a lion's share of the credit. His view is supported by the influential and eminent critic Richard Corliss, who includes Koch in his book *Talking Pictures* as one of the most important screenwriters in Hollywood history. Yet Julius Epstein (Philip died in 1952) has spent much of the past decade disput-ing Koch's claim and defending his and his brother's credit—not he says, for his benefit, but for his family's. "If it wasn't for the pressure from my kids and from my friends, I wouldn't have even been inter-ested," says Julius, who has not made a similar fuss about his other credits, including *Yankee Doodle Dandy*.

So how much did the Epsteins write? How much did Koch write? Where does the assertion of another Warners man, Casey Robinson, fit in? How much was taken from the play the movie was adapted from, *Everybody Comes to Rick's*? And since filmmaking is a collaborative process, it would be foolish not to expect director Michael Curtiz, the leading actors, and producer Hal Wallis to have played some sort of role in revising the script.

What's known for certain is that the Epsteins started writing a screenplay for *Casablanca* in the middle of February 1942. Two other Warners writers, Aeneas McKenzie and Wally Kline (whose best-known credit is the script for *They Died with Their Boots On*, with Errol Flynn as George Armstrong Custer) had spent the first six weeks of 1942 developing a script from the play. It's not clear whether the Epsteins had read the play; they likely worked exclusively from the McKenzie-Kline script. This adaptation is almost never mentioned in most accounts of the screenplay dispute, and the duo did not get any on-screen credit (although their salaries are included in the movie's budget). Yet the filmed script follows the outline of the play fairly closely, which begs still another question: How much of the final product did McKenzie and Kline write?

This is about the last time everyone agrees on what happened. The Epsteins, shortly after getting the assignment from Wallis, went to Washington sometime in January to work on the World War II *Why We Fight* documentary series directed by Frank Capra. But Wallis and Jack Warner made them promise they would work on the *Casablanca* script while they were in Washington. Julius Epstein says they didn't write a word before going to Washington, started on the script there, and then started again on their return to Hollywood four weeks later. When they returned, they were presented with thirty to forty pages written by Howard Koch.

Koch tells an entirely different story. When he was assigned to the picture April 6 (a date that is supported by documents in the Warners archives), he was given thirty to forty pages that he says were written by the Epsteins. The dates make Koch's story more plausible—if he didn't start working on the screenplay until the first week of April, it would have been difficult for him to write what Epstein says he wrote in time to be given to the Epsteins on their return. On the other hand, the Epsteins could have written that much since the middle of February, even allow-ing for their trip. A script dated April 2—before Koch was put on the picture—has been credited to the Epsteins by historian Rudy Behlmer. This script, says historian Ronald Haver, was used for pre-production planning: deciding what kind of sets to build, writing a budget, design-ing costumes, and the like.

It's important to learn who wrote the first third of the screenplay because that sets the tone for the rest of the debate. If the Epsteins wrote it, ironically, it probably adds more credence to Julius's claim that he

ILSA: "WAS THAT CANNON FIRE?
OR WAS IT MY HEART POUNDING?"

and his brother were the principal authors. It's much easier, after all, to graft something onto a whole object—Koch's contributions to the Epstein's script—than it is to take a whole object, slice it up, rearrange it, and then paste it back together.

The Epsteins and Koch each worked on a screenplay, independently of each other, from the beginning of April until the middle of May. This, too was not an unusual way of doing things, and it also wouldn't have been unusual for each writing team to think that their script was going to be used at the expense of the other. Lenore Coffee, for instance, who was nominated for an Academy Award for Best Screenplay with Julius Epstein in 1938 for *Four Daughters*, told an interviewer she had never met Epstein. They had worked independently, and then someone else (or even Coffee or Epstein, for that matter), put the final script together.

The revised screenplay was not finished when shooting started on May 25, which accounts for one of the legends surrounding the film. Koch, in his two books, gives the impression that he was racing against the clock to finish the script. Bogart was going to have to leave at summer's end to start filming *Sahara* at Columbia as part of a loan-out. Meanwhile, Curtiz was running out of pages to shoot, and the cast was getting surly about getting their lines moments before scenes were shot. The best description of the situation, and the one most widely quoted, is in Ingrid Bergman's autobiography:

"So every day we were shooting off the cuff; every day, they were handing out the dialogue, and we were trying to make some sense of it. No one knew where the picture was going, and no one knew how it was going to end."

But it may not have been quite that way. What is not included in the accepted version are the two sentences from Bergman's book before that: "From the very start, Hal Wallis, the producer, was arguing with the writers, the Epstein brothers and Howard Koch, and every lunchtime Mike Curtiz argued with Hal Wallis."

The problem, then, was not that there wasn't a script, but that there wasn't a script that Wallis, who had taken personal control of the production, liked. Koch wrote that about half of the 130-page script was written by May 25, but there had to have been more pages completed than that. There was the budget script, for one, and there is another memo from Koch to Wallis, dated May 11, where he implies he has one third of the script left to finish.

The director and cast were waiting for pages because Wallis was holding them up. This would account for the debates with the writers, which had started long before shooting began and continued after it started. Koch and Wallis would join Curtiz at his ranch on Sundays, spread script pages on the table and floor, and try to piece pages from different versions together.

Others besides Bergman have noted that both the Epsteins and Koch had problems sorting out various twists in the story. No one was satisfied with the romance parts of the screenplay. Bergman, for one, was mystified as to how to play her part. Should Ilsa look at Victor Laszlo with love, or should she look at Rick Blaine with love? Curtiz told her not to worry. "Just play it . . . in-between," he said. Wallis, too, didn't think the screenplays which had been written gave any good reasons why Rick and Ilsa should love each other (which, given Holly-wood's traditional disregard for plot logic, seems astounding). In fact, he was so unhappy with the way the Epsteins and Koch had written the love triangle that he assigned Robinson to the movie shortly after shooting began.

Bogart was unhappy with his role as it had been written in the play and in early drafts of the screenplay. The Rick Blaine of the play is motivated by revenge. He wants to get even with Ilsa for dumping him. The first drafts of the screenplay had kept this attitude. The early Rick Blaine was an American lawyer who had divorced his wife, abandoned his children, and slept with loose women. This is not the kind of character an audience would empathize with. Bogart wanted someone more like Sam Spade in *The Maltese Falcon*: "Don't be too sure I'm as crooked as I'm supposed to be." Both Koch and Julius Epstein say Bogart spent long periods of time discussing this with each of them, and his lobbying showed up in the shooting script. That Rick doesn't want revenge; he just wants to be left alone. Koch, the most political of the two, added the lines about running guns to the Ethiopians against the Italians and fighting with the Spanish Republicans against Franco. The Epsteins wrote the Captain Renault bit about Rick's past: "I'd like to think that you killed a man. It's the romantic in me."

Henreid had just as many doubts about Victor Laszlo. His aversion

RICK: "TELL ME, WHO WAS IT YOU LEFT ME FOR?
WAS IT LASZLO OR WERE THERE OTHERS IN
BETWEEN? OR AREN'T YOU THE KIND THAT TELLS?"

to white suits has been mentioned, but that was only the beginning of his complaints. He thought the early Epstein drafts were "dreadful," and had to be coerced into participating by Koch and another writer, Albert Maltz, who outlined the movie to him in much the same way the Epsteins bluffed David O. Selznick into lending Bergman. In fact, Henreid says that Maltz wrote much of the Laszlo part, and he was surprised Koch got screen credit instead of Maltz. Even after shooting began, Henreid threatened to walk out if he didn't get Bergman at the end, and he was especially unhappy with the famous "Marseillaise" scene. Laszlo, wearing his white suit, leads the cafe's band in the French national anthem and drowns out a group of German soldiers singing "Die Wacht am Rhein," a German military song. The key moment in the scene is when the house band looks at Rick, who nods his approval. "I am described by the Germans as a great leader of the masses," Henreid wrote in his autobiography, "a man who can command obedience. That's the reason the Germans don't want me to leave Casablanca. After the rehearsal, I asked Curtiz, 'What the hell is going on? Why do they look away and then back at me? I'm supposed to be a leader of the masses, and here I have a stinking little band, and I can't get them to do what I want!'"

Finally, there was the ending, which continued to stump everyone—Wallis, the Epsteins, Koch, and Robinson. This is where the truth comes closest to matching the *Casablanca* legend. The writers, Curtiz, and Wallis weren't sure what should happen: Does Ilsa go off with Laszlo or stay with Rick? Does Rick get away after helping Laszlo and Ilsa escape, does he end up in a French prison, or is he killed? "Philip and I could never figure out the ending until just before the last week of shooting," Julius said in 1988. "I remember we were driving Michael Curtiz insane."

As the end of shooting approached, no decision had been reached, and everyone who was there agrees Wallis and Curtiz had decided to film two endings for the love story. They would pick one after showing each version to preview audiences. Meanwhile, although no one liked it, they had decided to settle for the play's resolution, in which Rick is arrested. No one had a better idea until the Epsteins were brainstorming one day as they were driving down Sunset Boulevard. That's when Renault's conversion to patriotism offered a way out—they would move the scene to the airport, where Laszlo would get away (with or without Ilsa) and Renault would cover for Rick. This new ending was the final scene filmed. Curtiz shot the Ilsa/Laszlo and Rick/Renault version first, and it seemed so natural that the second, Rick/Ilsa ending was never filmed.

A version with the Ilsa/Laszlo ending, with Rick getting arrested, was published in a 1944 screenplay anthology. It takes place at Rick's cafe (where the play also concludes), and Rick gives the letters of transit to Laszlo. This version does not include the "hill of beans" speech between Rick and Ilsa, and Rick holds a gun on Renault while the camera cuts back and forth between the cafe and the airport, where Ilsa and Laszlo are getting on the plane. After the plane buzzes over the cafe, Rick surrenders, and Renault and Strasser take him to jail.

This is a weak ending, and there are several reasons to believe Koch wrote it. A draft of a Koch script has an ending similar to this published version (which includes the aforementioned chess scene between Rick and Renault). Equally as important are Warners employment records that show that Koch was taken off the picture two weeks after filming started, while the Epsteins weren't taken off for another week. If Koch had completed his version of the script, it makes sense he would be given another movie to work on. Remember, a contract writer rarely stayed with a movie from start to finish. It's possible a writer could be called back, and Behlmer says Koch was to work on the airport ending (although the dates he gives don't seem to match). But once their part of the picture was finished, they moved on to their next assignment.

More importantly, the cafe ending helps to buttress the Epsteins' claim. Julius says they didn't come up with the ending that was used in the final print until the last week of shooting (which explains why the wrong version was published in the 1944 anthology). That fits the time frame above: The Epsteins worked on the movie a week longer than Koch did, which would have been when they wrote the airport ending. And if Curtiz and Wallis kept them around to write the airport ending while dismissing Koch, it's not hard to believe that Curtiz and Wallis trusted their judgment on the rest of the script as well.

There is one more piece of evidence that casts doubt on Koch's claim. If Wallis and Curtiz were satisfied with Koch's script, why did Wallis assign Robinson—one of the studio's best writers and one of Wallis's favorites—to the picture? Again, the time frame is important. Robinson started work at about the same time as shooting began, and worked on the script for about three weeks—as long as the Epsteins did and one week longer than Koch. The only explanation is that he was revising parts of the Koch script, since the Epsteins were still working on their script. Robinson, who told an interviewer in 1974 that he had urged Wallis to buy *Everybody Comes to Rick's*, says he worked on the love scenes between Rick and Ilsa. He apparently recommended much of the action in the second part of the "Play it again, Sam" scene, when Ilsa comes to the cafe, and the "You'll have to do the thinking for both of us" scene in Rick's apartment while Laszlo is at the underground meeting. But the differences between his recommendations and the final print indicate it's likely someone else wrote the scenes that were eventually filmed. For instance, in Robinson's description of how the screenplay was written, the scene between Rick and Ilsa that takes place in the bazaar ("For special friends of Rick's we have a special discount") takes place in Rick's apartment.

And who could have taken Robinson's scenes and fit them into the script that had been written? None other than the Epsteins, who had been working on the movie longer than any of the other writers, and who consequently had the best vision of what the whole should be made up of. And if they could do that for the Robinson material, why couldn't they have done it for Koch's material? Julius Epstein says Koch didn't write more than one-third of the final screenplay, which is an interesting assertion. He's very specific, and much more specific than Koch (who is rather circumspect about the matter). Granted, Epstein could have made the figure up, but his reputation is so sterling (even Wallis, who didn't much care for the Epsteins, doesn't bad mouth them in his book) that it's likely there's some truth behind it. It also doesn't hurt the Epsteins' claim that their forte, as even Koch acknowledges, was witty dialogue—and Casablanca has more witty dialogue in one scene than most movies have in two hours.

Knowing all this, here's an educated guess about who really wrote Casablanca:

THE EPSTEINS did the majority of the work, writing the framework and incorporating some of the material from the other writers. Most of the dialogue that has become a part of film lore came from them, as did the airport ending—"Round up the usual suspects." "The studio knows who did what," Julius said in 1983. "They made us producers. . . . They gave us a new contract. They gave us a whole bungalow with fireplaces." It is interesting to note that he and his brother were each paid four times what Koch was paid to work on the movie.

KOCH wrote much of the political material, emphasizing Rick's anti-fascist past. He was probably responsible, with Maltz's cooperation, of building up the Laszlo part in scenes like the one after the Underground meeting—"If we stop breathing, we'll die. If we stop fighting our enemies, the world will die."

ROBINSON played an important role in clarifying Ilsa's dilemma, especially in the Paris flashback. His description of the climactic apartment scene differs little from what was used. But some of his material was probably rewritten by others, including Koch.

CURTIZ, whose contribution is too often overlooked, is credited by several cast members with combining pages from various scripts, and then shooting the results. He also suggested beefing up the Strasser role to provide a clear-cut villain (which was done), and volunteered several vignettes about refugees (which were used).

THE CAST, as mentioned, influenced their roles by making suggestions to the various writers. This wasn't unusual then, and it's even less unusual now.

WALLIS wrote the movie's final line—"Louis, I think this is the beginning of a beautiful friendship." But it's likely he had much, much more to do with the screenplay than that. One critic has gone so far as to suggest that Wallis was *Casablanca*'s *auteur*, or creative force: that his direction shaped everything from the lighting to the publicity. The finished movie is almost surely the Epsteins' script filtered through Curtiz's camera and Wallis's vision.

Also overlooked is the contribution of **MURRAY BURNETT** and **JOAN ALISON,** who wrote the play. Author Aljean Harmetz contends that there's more of the play in the movie than anyone has realized—the characters, the plot outline, and the idea of the letters of transit. The play also contains a version of the "Play it again, Sam" scene and the phrase, "Here's looking at you, kid."

Finally, don't forget **THE CENSORS.** Movies in 1941 were reviewed by an agency whose duty was to excise all of the naughtiness, and the censors did their job with a vengeance. Many of Captain Renault's double entendres that are in the published 1944 shooting script were deleted by the censors.

You Must Remember This

TRIVIA INTERLUDE #3

WHEN RICK HELPS THE YOUNG BULGARIAN COUPLE WIN THE MONEY FOR THEIR EXIT VISA, WHAT ROULETTE NUMBER DOES HE TELL JAN TO BET ON?

00
17
22
35

22.

WHAT BRAND OF CIGARETTES DOES RICK BLAINE SMOKE?

Camel
Lucky Strike
Chesterfield
Marlboro

Chesterfield. It isn't mentioned in the movie, but that's what Humphrey Bogart smoked—and smoking's what killed him. He died of throat cancer.

MATCH THESE LEGENDARY LINES OF DIALOGUE WITH THE CHARACTER WHO SAYS THEM:

1. "I bet they're asleep in New York. I bet they're asleep all over America."
2. "You know, Rick, I have many friends in Casablanca, but somehow just because you despise me, you are the only one I trust."
3. "As leader of all illegal activities in Casablanca, I'm an influential and respected man."
4. "Play it once, Sam, for old times' sake. . . . Play it, Sam. Play 'As Time Goes By.'"

5. "I have already given him the best, knowing he was German and would take it anyway."
6. "I know, for instance, that you're in love with a woman. It is perhaps a strange circumstance that we should both love the same woman."
7. "Well, we mustn't underestimate American blundering. I was with them when they blundered into Berlin in 1918."

1. Rick 2. Ugarte 3. Ferrari 4. Ilsa 5. Carl 6. Laszlo 7. Renault

HOW MANY LANGUAGES ARE SPOKEN IN CASABLANCA?

Six. English, French, Italian, Spanish, Japanese, and German.

MATCH THESE CHARACTERS WITH THEIR NATIONALITIES:

1. Sacha	a. Norwegian
2. Carl	b. Bulgarian
3. Laszlo	c. Russian
4. Berger	d. German
5. Annina	e. Czech

Sacha/Russian; Carl/German; Laszlo/Czech; Berger/Norwegian; Annina/Bulgarian.

CASABLANCA WAS SHOT ON WARNER BROS.' BACK LOT, BUT THAT DIDN'T STOP THE STUDIO FROM USING A VARIETY OF "LOCATIONS" IN THE MOVIE. HOW MANY DIFFERENT PLACES ARE IN THE MOVIE, AND WHAT ARE THEY?

Seven. The airport, Rick's Café Américain, Laszlo's hotel, the bazaar, the Blue Parrot, the prefect's office, and Paris (in the flashback sequence).

Who's Who in Casablanca

THE WRITERS

Julius J. Epstein (b. August 22, 1909, New York City) is sick and tired of *Casablanca*. "I get this phone call from a woman, a USC film student," he told an interviewer in 1988, "and she's writing a paper on—guess what?—*Four Daughters? Fanny? Pete 'n' Tillie?* Forty-seven pictures I've done—and all they ask about is this goddamn *Casablanca*."

Epstein has a point—up to a point. He and his identical twin, **Philip G.** (b. August 22, 1909, New York City; d. February 7, 1952, Los Angeles), were contract writers at Warner Bros. for seventeen years, and during their tenure either wrote, adapted, or doctored some of the studio's best scripts. Their work included melodramas (*Mr. Skeffington*), musicals (*Yankee Doodle Dandy*), and comedies (*The Man Who Came to Dinner*). After Philip died of cancer, Julius's solo career continued through the end of the studio system, the advent of television, and the big-budget, special-effects Hollywood of the 1980s. He was nominated for an Academy Award for Best Screenplay for *Reuben, Reuben* in 1983 (one of four Oscar nominations) at the age of seventy-four. He also earned a Writers Guild Lifetime Achievement Award in 1955 (even though his career still had twenty-five years and two Oscar nominations to go).

But that stuff is for film buffs. *Casablanca* is for everybody, which is something Julius Epstein has never quite come to grips with. He once called the movie "slick shit," which will not endear him to anyone who gets a lump in their throat during the final airport scene. "I don't hate it," he said in the same interview, but added that "there wasn't one moment of reality in *Casablanca*."

It also wasn't the sort of picture that the Epsteins usually worked on. In retrospect, they probably weren't suited for it, and may have been assigned to it because of their skill at adapting plays to the screen. The Epsteins' skills were best used in sophisticated comedy, and Julius's favorite writers were people like Philip Barry (who wrote the play *The Philadelphia Story*) and English humorist P. G. Wodehouse. Those are hardly the influences political love stories are made of. But it didn't stop them from realizing that Renault, a part Julius said they wrote for Claude Rains, could be a drawing room comic as well as a sleazy cop.

83

LASZLO: "I SLEPT VERY WELL."

RENAULT: "THAT'S STRANGE. NOBODY'S SUPPOSED
TO SLEEP WELL IN CASABLANCA."

The Epsteins were born in the Jewish slum on New York's Lower East Side; their father ran a livery stable but made a good enough living so that Julius and Philip graduated from college. Julius went to Hollywood in 1933 as a ghostwriter for a college classmate, Jerry Wald. The legend says Wald (who shows up in almost every book about Hollywood as the ultimate filmland character) had sold a script but didn't know how to write one. He wired Julius to come and bail him out, and Epstein stayed. He is still there. Philip, meanwhile, came out a year later, and their first shared screen credit came in 1939 for *Daughters Courageous*, directed by Michael Curtiz and starring Rains and John Garfield.

HOWARD KOCH (b. December 12, 1902, New York City) became a screenwriter because he was a lousy lawyer. In his autobiography, he says he would sit in his office tinkering with scripts from plays instead of drumming up business. An inauspicious debut, but it would lead to an association with Orson Welles, William Wyler, Jean Negulesco, Howard Hawks, John Huston, Max Ophuls, and the House Un-American Activities Committee.

Koch gave up lawyering in the mid-1930s after trying to establish a practice in upstate New York. He wrote several plays that were performed by the New Deal's Federal Theater project before he stumbled on a job as a contract writer for Welles's Mercury Theater. In 1938, says Koch, Welles came to him and said he wanted to do a Halloween radio broadcast about an alien invasion of the Earth. The result was "The War of the Worlds" and its resultant panic, and it led, two years later, to Koch's first Hollywood credit.

Koch's movie career, which besides *Casablanca* included *The Letter*, *Letter From an Unknown Woman*, and an Academy Award nomination for *Sergeant York*, eventually revolved around a movie he wrote in 1943 called *Mission to Moscow*. It was based on the book of the same name by Joseph Davies, a former United States ambassador to the Soviet Union. The movie, a piece of World War II propaganda, was likely made with the approval of high-ranking federal officials, although not that of President Roosevelt (as Jack Warner was fond of boasting).

In the movie, Davies extolled the virtues of Soviet dictator Joseph

Stalin. "There is no man in the world I would trust more fully," he once said. This probably didn't seem silly during the middle of the war.

But it seemed a lot sillier, and much more subversive, in 1947 when J. Parnell Thomas brought HUAC to Hollywood to look for communists under the bed. The subject has been covered admirably in Walter Goodman's *The Committee*, a riveting account of HUAC in all its incarnations between the end of World War II and Vietnam; sufficient for these purposes is noting that Koch was one of the nineteen writers and directors Thomas's panel suspected of being a Red. Their evidence was *Mission to Moscow*, as well as a number of left-wing causes Koch had supported.

Koch never testified, since Thomas ended the hearings before he got his chance. He subsequently missed becoming a member of the immortal Hollywood Ten—the $2,000-a-week writers who took the First Amendment when asked if they belonged to the Communist Party (their salaries being an irony that no one seemed to notice at the time). All ten went to jail for contempt of Congress and were blacklisted in Hollywood for another decade or so. Koch, too, was blacklisted, although it has never been illegal in the United States to belong to the Communist Party. He moved to Europe when he couldn't get work in the United States, where he wrote and produced several pictures in the late 1950s and early 1960s under the pseudonym of Peter Howard.

There are a number of delicious morsels about Koch's blacklisting, although there's no doubt they weren't too tasty at the time. The first, of course, is that he was a contract writer. If he had turned down *Mission to Moscow*, he would have been suspended. Second, he seems to have been the only one associated with the movie who was blacklisted. Studio boss Warner, who signed up the book, was not only not blacklisted, but served as a friendly witness and named names. Curtiz, who directed, was not blacklisted; neither were Walter Huston, who played Davies, and Eleanor Parker, who became a big star in the next decade. Not much is known about Parker's politics, but Huston was no Ronald Reagan conservative. Of course, it didn't hurt that his son John (who led the main protest against the blacklisting) was one of the top-grossing directors of the era. Money has always talked in Hollywood, even during scoundrel time.

Everybody Comes to Rick's

Hollywood stops for no man. The Japanese bombed Pearl Harbor on December 7, 1941, but the next day, Stephen Karnot showed up for work at Warner Bros. He was a story analyst, and his job that Monday was to start reading a play called *Everybody Comes to Rick's*.

Karnot read the play over the next four days, and it must have been difficult for him to concentrate on the love life of an American exile in French Morocco who followed a neutral foreign policy when residents of the West Coast expected to be invaded at any minute. But he persevered, and his 61-line, single-spaced synopsis still exists in the Warners archives.

Karnot (who, in one of those great movie twists of fate, immediately fades from the scene after this moment in front of the camera) thought the play an excellent melodrama. He liked the tight plotting, tense mood, and "sophisticated hokum." He recommended Bogart to play against Mary Astor.

Warners had bought *Everybody Comes to Rick's*, as previously mentioned, for $20,000 from the New York playwrights Murray Burnett and Joan Alison. In 1938, Burnett traveled to Europe, where his itinerary included a stop in Brussels to help his wife's relatives emigrate to the United States and a pause in Vienna shortly after the Nazi occupation of Austria. In Vienna, Burnett got a firsthand look at the hospitality the Nazis extended to their guests (one reason why his wife's relatives were leaving); in Vienna and later in the south of France, he learned about the refugee trail that the movie's opening montage describes. It was in the south of France that he stumbled upon the nightclub with the black piano player, whose audience included Nazis, Frenchmen, and refugees.

Two years later, Burnett and Alison wrote a play about Rick Blaine, an American lawyer who divorces his wife and abandons his children to open a cafe in Casablanca in French Morocco. They incorporated much of what Burnett had learned during their summer in Europe, and tied it in with World War II and the month-old German conquest of France. The play includes:

A BLACK PIANO PLAYER named Sam, who is the only person who knows what is in, as Karnot put it, Rick's embittered heart. This was a daring cast move in 1940, when few plays were integrated.

A plot that centers around some LETTERS OF TRANSIT, which will allow a wealthy Czech resistance leader to flee Casablanca one step ahead of the Nazis. The Czech, Victor Laszlo, is traveling with an American woman of mystery named Lois Meredith—who just happens to be the woman who broke Rick's heart in Paris. Rick had fled Paris after learning that Lois was living with another man (not Laszlo) while she was having an affair with Rick. He had come across Lois and her boyfriend in a Paris cafe called La Belle Aurore. Wallis, with advice from Casey Robinson, apparently made the decision that changed American Lois Meredith to Norwegian Ilsa Lund.

A CORRUPT VICHY POLICE OFFICIAL, Luis Rinaldo, and A YOUNG GESTAPO OFFICIAL, Heinrich Strasser. Rinaldo, of course, was changed to Renault in the movie (in either the McKenzie-Kline draft or an early Epstein script), while Strasser's minor role in the play became the movie's main villain.

A SECOND PLOT LINE featuring a Bulgarian émigré couple, Jan and Annina Viereck. The Vierecks become entangled with Rick, Lois, and Laszlo when Rick hides them from Rinaldo. Rinaldo had tried to seduce Annina, and Jan had hit the prefect. The Vierecks then use the second letter of transit to escape Casablanca. The Vierecks all but vanish from the movie, save for the scene where Rick lets Jan win at roulette.

AN ENDING that sees Rick send Lois off with Laszlo (with the other letter of transit) while he stays at the cafe and covers Rinaldo and Strasser with a gun. Lois had tried to get the letters of transit from Rick by sleeping with him; in the end, Rick is motivated not by sex but by his renewed self-respect. This is not all that different from the Epsteins' ending (and even more similar to the published 1944 ending), and lends some credence to the theory that Burnett and Alison are responsible for more of the screenplay than they get credit for.

The play is not, as critic James Agee called it in *The Nation*, "one of the world's worst." It has some creaky moments—the lights go out after Jan clobbers Rinaldo—but it probably deserved to be produced. What happened is that the Broadway producers who optioned it were leery of the sexual content of the play, and asked Burnett and Alison to rewrite it to make it less obvious that Lois prostitutes herself to get the letters of transit. This was, after all, 1941. Burnett and Alison refused (how different would Hollywood history have been if they had agreed?), and their agent offered the play to several studios in Hollywood. That's when Wallis and Jack Warner, looking for a followup to *Algiers* and ever watchful for properties that followed the headlines, bought it.

Or, if Casey Robinson is to be believed, that's when *he* tried to buy it. Robinson said in a series of interviews (part of the American Film Institute's Oral History Project) that he came across a copy of the play during a train trip he made with Wallis. "[The play]," Robinson said, "was set in Casablanca, Africa, and there the relationship with the picture almost ends." This is not true, which may cast some doubt on the rest of Robinson's story. He says he then sent a telegram to the Warners agent in New York—in Wallis's name—asking for the play's purchase price. Wallis was intrigued with Robinson's action, and eventually bought the play based on Robinson's enthusiasm.

The Fundamental Things Apply
QUICK TAKES #3

◆ Koch and Curtiz had several disagreements about the script during shooting, including one when Koch was adamant that the flashback scene was a waste of time. "In retrospect, I suspect Mike was right," he wrote in 1979. Another time, Koch was protesting about what he considered the illogical changes Curtiz wanted to make in the script. "Don't worry what's logical," Curtiz told him. "I make it go so fast no one notices."

◆ The threatening letter from the Warner Bros.' legal department undoubtedly sent Groucho Marx into a comic fit in 1946, when he and his brothers were filming *A Night in Casablanca*. Groucho wrote back: "I had no idea that the city of Casablanca belonged exclusively to Warner Bros. . . . You probably have the right to use the name Warners, but what about Brothers? Professionally, we were brothers long before you were." Groucho got his revenge several years later when Warners announced plans for *Night and Day*, a biography of Cole Porter. Groucho immediately threatened a lawsuit of his own, writing that it was obvious the studio was infringing on the Marxes' *A Night at the Opera* and *A Day at the Races*.

◆ Several critics have noted that Rick seems to be devastated by an affair that lasted just weeks and had been over for eighteen months, from the fall of France in June 1940 to December 1941. This, they point out, hardly seems long enough to store up a great deal of resentment. The disparity comes from the play, where Rick and Lois have not seen each other in four years and where their affair lasted much longer. When Koch superimposed Rick's past over the structure of the play—running guns in 1935, fighting in Spain in 1936, spying in Paris in 1939–40—he didn't pay any attention to the play's time structure.

◆ Several scenes that are in the published 1944 version but were cut from the final print explained the background of the minor characters. Sacha, for instance, was the czar's favorite sword swallower, and Carl was a mathematics professor from Liepzig (which, using Hollywood logic, explains why he gets to keep Rick's financial accounts).

◆ Woody Allen, a *Casablanca* scholar of some renown, has no doubts about who wrote the movie. There are numerous references to Julius Epstein in Allen's films. A psychoanalyst in one movie is named Julius Epstein, another character has a nameplate that says Epstein. The idea of the wedding night play-by-play in *Bananas* is lifted from a column Epstein ghostwrote for Wald when the latter was a New York newspaper columnist, a play-by-play account of an appendectomy.

The End

#3

Murray Burnett who turned eighty in 1991, remains adamant about what he considers his unfair treatment by Warner Bros. "I still have a great deal of hatred for them," he says. "Warners has consistently downgraded the play. They won't even tell anyone there was a play."

The dispute, not surprisingly, centers around money. Warners made a lot of it from *Casablanca*, and Burnett hasn't seen a penny since his 1941 payoff. This galls him, even though his life didn't end after

Everybody Comes to Rick's became the world's least-known famous play. Burnett worked for many years for the Corporation for Entertainment and Learning, a New York company that produced the Bill Moyers "Walk Through the 20th Century" television programs.

Much of the problem with Warners, as Burnett acknowledges, is that he signed the contract willingly. He didn't pay enough attention ("and neither did my agent, who was no good") to the clause in the contract that assigned all of the play's rights—including those not yet invented—to Warners in perpetuity. This meant that not only did Burnett not get a share of any money the film made, but he didn't get to share in the receipts from video cassette sales, television rights, and the like. That video and TV didn't exist then was irrelevant. Burnett also lost the rights to the characters, which meant he couldn't use Rick Blaine in another play.

In 1983 Burnett sued to recover some of that money. The lawsuit dragged through the courts for several years before it was dismissed.

But Burnett got a modicum of revenge when he was working for CEL. A man he met who worked near his Manhattan office told Burnett he didn't believe *Casablanca* was based on a play. When Burnett insisted that it was, and that he had written it, the man still refused to believe him. Finally, they bet $50. Burnett went home, got a copy of *Everyone Comes to Rick's*, returned, and pocketed the man's money.

Did he notice the look on the man's face when he came back with the play? "No," says Burnett. "The only thing I wanted to see was his money."

*N*o one has ever accused Hollywood executives of being concerned with anything more than profit-and-loss statements.

That's why it shouldn't be surprising to learn there were few people in Hollywood who had something nice to say about *Casablanca* before it was made. There are pages and pages and pages written and spoken about the pre-production and production processes, and almost all of it is negative.

Paul Henreid threatened to go on suspension rather than play Victor Laszlo. Michael Curtiz was running around the set in a constant fit, terrified he would make a bad picture and ruin his reputation. Bergman, who was not used to the Warners assembly line, was mystified and a little scared of a process that provided her with her lines only hours before she had to speak them. Hal Wallis had to fend off not only the writers, director, and cast, but also Jack Warner, who first wanted to remake *Algiers*, and then wanted to use every Warners male lead except Humphrey Bogart. Julius Epstein didn't think it was anything special then, and he thinks even less of it now.

Perhaps the best line came from a Warners contract writer named Robert Buckner (whose *Yankee Doodle Dandy* screenplay was rewritten by the Epsteins). He read the play, and wrote in his report that not only did he dislike it intensely, but that "its big moment is sheer hokum melodrama . . . and this guy Rick is two parts Hemingway, one part Scott Fitzgerald and a dash of cafe Christ."

FERRARI: "AH. THE NEWS ABOUT UGARTE

UPSETS ME VERY MUCH."

RICK: "YOU'RE A FAT HYPOCRITE. YOU DON'T FEEL ANY SORRIER FOR UGARTE THAN I DO."

So much for one of the cultural icons of the second half of the twentieth century.

To be fair, much of the uncertainty is understandable. The studio's skepticism, from the bosses to the actors to the key grip, can no doubt be credited to everyone's familiarity with a process that was rushed, harried, and aggravating—something that was almost guaranteed to breed contempt. It's difficult, during production, to tell if even an *ordinary* movie is going to be good. And *Casablanca* was no ordinary movie. It's even more understandable given the nature of large bureaucracies (and Warners, like the other studios, was just that): No one is going to say something nice about a proposal when the easiest thing to do is to say something nasty. People get fired for pushing something that fails, not by knocking something that eventually becomes a success.

What no one working on the Warners back lot fifty years ago could possibly have known is that *Casablanca* is the perfect Hollywood film. And that's just not the opinion of a besotted Casablanquiste (to borrow a term from Maurice Zolotow's 1988 interview with Epstein) who owned the movie soundtrack when he was in junior high school; try this from Leonard Maltin, the editor of the essential *TV Movies*: "Our candidate for best Hollywood movie of all time."

Or any of these testimonials:
♦ From Pulitzer Prize-winning critic Roger Ebert, who named *Casablanca* as one of the ten best movies ever for a 1982 survey: "[I picked it] because of its perfect marriage of time and place and character and that song that Dooley Wilson doesn't think he quite remembers."
♦ From a 1988 survey of twenty-two critics across the world: ninth among the one hundred best movies of all time.
♦ From Leslie Halliwell, author of the groundbreaking *Filmgoer's Companion*: "Deserved and kept its fame for its witty script, polished direction, and lustrous star and supporting performances."
♦ From the 1977 American Film Institute Poll of the top ten American films of all time: third, behind *Gone With the Wind* and *Citizen Kane*.
♦ From critic Richard Corliss: "Like the very best Hollywood films but unlike the works by the European commercial avant-garde, *Casablanca* succeeds as allegory, popular myth, clinical psychology, or whatever, and as a superb romantic melodrama."
♦ From a 1972 USC poll of the most significant movies in American

cinema history: eighteenth among the fifty-three named by a panel of film producers and critics. A 1977 *TV Guide* poll revealed it was the most popular, frequently shown film on television. From a 1975 poll of 1,500 film and television industry executives: Second among the top thirty vote-getters.

◆ From Hollywood historian Charles Higham: "Yet here is one cult movie that deserves its reputation. It will soon be [fifty] years old, but it continues to exert an appeal even on those too young to have received its initial impact."

There are certainly more critically acclaimed movies in the history of the medium, and there are certainly more artistically important. *Citizen Kane*, directed by Orson Welles, is always held up as the example of what Hollywood can do when it wants to make meaningful movies (though it was ignored when released); there are any number of European films, directed by people like Jean-Luc Godard and Ingmar Bergman, that can be dissected as works of art.

There's art in *Casablanca*, but it is not a work of art. There is filmmaking in *Casablanca*, but it's not a filmmaker's film. Not only are there no sensitive older women to teach a young boy the facts of life, but a visionary like Welles probably would have cast Charlton Heston as Rick, and then told him to play the role with a Mexican accent (see *Touch of Evil*).

Casablanca displays all of the skills that Hollywood's producers, directors, and actors developed to make the town the movie capital of the world sixty years ago and have used to keep it there ever since. It has a plot with a beginning, middle, and end—a narrative style that in many ways is unique to American films. It has characters that the audience can identify with, and a technique many foreign filmmakers don't consider especially important and foreign audiences don't expect. And it moves—crisply, professionally, expertly—from beginning to end, with hardly a pause that would allow the audience time to reflect on the action. In contrast, try to imagine a Bergman film that didn't give its viewers a moment to think about the director's thesis. No one may ever have explained it better than a college student interviewed outside of a New York City theater showing a Bogart festival in 1965: "I'm tired of those Italian films where everybody justs sits around and has boring parties."

Casablanca owes much of its present-day popularity to filmgoers like that student, who would become part of a new generation of Casablanquistes. Though the movie was a success when first released, and won three Academy Awards, it became just another wartime movie that seemed increasingly irrelevant in a country preoccupied with other things in the "Father Knows Best"/McCarthy witch-hunt 1950s. Remember, too, that there were few opportunities to see the film in that era. Home video hadn't been invented, and television was not the place to see old movies that still had an appeal at the box office; *Casablanca* was re-released to theaters several times after 1942.

Two things happened to revive interest in *Casablanca*: Bogart died in 1957, and art houses and repertory theaters became increasingly popular. Bogart's death, for better or worse, deified the actor. Instead of a balding, splotchy-faced leading man who drank too much and whose last couple of pictures were a mixed bag of winners, losers, and duds (no one appreciated *Beat the Devil* at the time, Bogart included), he became a symbol in a way that none of his contemporaries have. Spencer Tracy, Gary Cooper, Cary Grant, and Clark Gable were just as popular, but when's the last time a theater held a Cooper film festival? That interest is something the art houses, many located on or near college campuses, noticed. After the studios sold their movie theaters in the 1950s to settle the federal antitrust lawsuit, and it became possible for independent theater owners to stay in business, they still needed something to show. And what better to show than old movies, which could be rented less expensively than first-run films and were like first-run films to audiences that hadn't seen them before?

One of the first, if not *the* first, art houses to discover *Casablanca*'s appeal to a new generation of moviegoers was the Brattle Theater in Cambridge, Massachusetts, the home of Harvard University. The Brattle became an art house in 1953, and almost immediately began showing Bogart films. It held its first Bogart Event in the late 1950s, and continued the annual festivals for much of the next decade. The Brattle is the theater where, a horrified Ingrid Bergman once told Dick Cavett, the audience knew every line in *Casablanca* by heart—so when the sound occasionally went off during the screening, the crowd picked up the dialogue. In 1964, some 15,000 people attended the Brattle's Bogart Festival, and the theater went so far as to open a Blue Parrot Cafe. Even today, despite several changes in ownership and a bankruptcy, the

98

RICK: "HAVE YOU TRIED 22 TONIGHT?"

Brattle continues to make Bogart films a staple of its programming. The centerpiece of the Brattle's 100th anniversary celebration in 1990 was, not surprisingly, *Casablanca*.

"I can explain [*Casablanca*'s] success only by the Bogie cult that has sprung up after his death," Julius Epstein said in 1980. He may have a point. Check newspaper and newsmagazine indexes in the mid-1960s, and it's impossible to miss the cult forming. In one month in 1965, four Manhattan theaters were hosting Bogart revivals; there were one thousand people in a theater built to seat eight hundred. Six books about Bogart were published that year, and each of them had a scene from *Casablanca* pictured somewhere on its cover. The appeal, according to Eugene Archer in *The New York Times*, was that "the world, [Bogart's] expression seemed to say, is no damn good, and there's not a damn thing you can do about it."

In retrospect, that's not hard to understand at all. The generation that discovered Bogart and *Casablanca* in 1965 needed something to believe in, for it certainly seemed as if the world was collapsing around it—Vietnam, race riots, and the rest. Bogart offered a code of conduct at a time when the proper conduct was becoming increasingly harder to discern. Compare that uncertainty and indecision with the situation in 1941, when Hitler and Naziism made it extremely simple to choose sides.

And that need for something to believe in didn't change when America left the 1960s, either. In the 1970s, it would be inflation, unemployment, and the Arab oil embargo. In the 1980s, it would be the savings and loan collapse, the environment, and the homeless. So why not believe in someone who realized "that the lives of three people don't amount to a hill of beans in this crazy world" and who always did the right thing, no matter how much it cost him to do it?

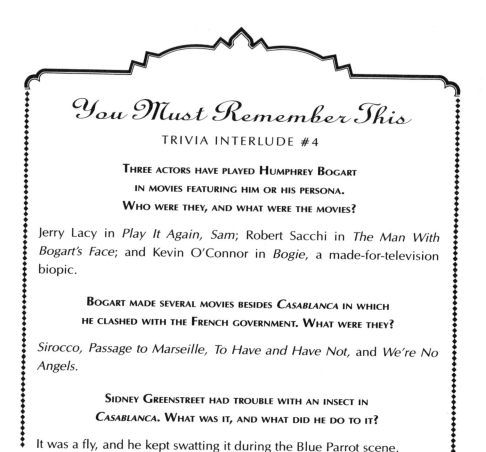

You Must Remember This

TRIVIA INTERLUDE #4

**THREE ACTORS HAVE PLAYED HUMPHREY BOGART
IN MOVIES FEATURING HIM OR HIS PERSONA.
WHO WERE THEY, AND WHAT WERE THE MOVIES?**

Jerry Lacy in *Play It Again, Sam*; Robert Sacchi in *The Man With Bogart's Face*; and Kevin O'Connor in *Bogie*, a made-for-television biopic.

**BOGART MADE SEVERAL MOVIES BESIDES *CASABLANCA* IN WHICH
HE CLASHED WITH THE FRENCH GOVERNMENT. WHAT WERE THEY?**

Sirocco, *Passage to Marseille*, *To Have and Have Not*, and *We're No Angels*.

**SIDNEY GREENSTREET HAD TROUBLE WITH AN INSECT IN
CASABLANCA. WHAT WAS IT, AND WHAT DID HE DO TO IT?**

It was a fly, and he kept swatting it during the Blue Parrot scene.

**WHAT IS UGARTE DOING WHEN HE IS
ARRESTED BY THE POLICE?**

Playing roulette.

**WINE, NOT SURPRISINGLY, PLAYS AN IMPORTANT ROLE IN A MOVIE
THAT TAKES PLACE PRIMARILY IN A BAR. WHAT KIND OF WINE IS IT?**

Champagne. Major Strasser orders champagne and caviar, Captain Re-
nault orders a bottle of the cafe's best champagne for Laszlo and Ilsa,
Laszlo and Berger drink champagne cocktails at the bar, and Rick and
Ilsa drink champagne constantly in the Paris flashback scene.

**DRINKING, IN FACT, IS COMMON THROUGHOUT THE FILM.
MATCH THESE CHARACTERS AND THEIR LIQUID OF CHOICE.**

1. Ferrari   a. Brandy
2. Rick   b. Bourbon
3. Yvonne   c. Coffee
4. Carl   d. Cognac

Ferrari/coffee; Rick/bourbon; Yvonne/cognac; Carl/brandy.

**THERE ARE TWO THINGS THAT RICK WON'T DO WITH CUSTOMERS
THAT HE DOES AFTER ILSA APPEARS. WHAT ARE THEY?**

He won't drink with customers, and he won't pick up a check.

**ALTHOUGH RENAULT LIKES GIRLS, HE IS NEVER SEEN WITH ANY.
YET THE PLOT DETAILS SEVERAL OF HIS PLANS TO SEDUCE
WOMEN, AND THERE IS EVEN A REFERENCE TO "A BEAUTIFUL YOUNG
GIRL FOR MONSIEUR RENAULT" DURING THE FIRST ROUNDUP
OF SUSPECTS AT THE BEGINNING OF THE FILM. HOW MANY WOMEN
DOES HE HAVE HIS EYE ON, AND WHO ARE THEY?**

Four. Yvonne, after Rick dumps her; Annina, so that she can get an exit
visa; "a breathtaking blonde" he plans to bring to the cafe (but never
does since the movie ends before he can); and "a visa problem" he
deals with in his office after his meeting with Strasser, Laszlo, and Ilsa.

Oscar Night

Does anyone remember an actor named Charles Coburn? They should, because according to the Academy of Motion Picture Arts and Sciences, he was the Best Supporting Actor in any movie released between December 1942 and November 1943 for his role in *The More the Merrier*.

To be fair, Coburn's performance in the picture—a comedy set in wartime Washington directed by George Stevens in which Jean Arthur shared an apartment with two men—wasn't bad. But how could anyone have voted for Coburn instead of Claude Rains, who was nominated for his performance as the marvelously slimy Louis Renault? And how, for that matter, could Ingrid Bergman have been nominated as Best Actress for *For Whom the Bell Tolls* and not for *Casablanca*?

Casablanca was nominated for eight Oscars: Best Picture, Best Director, Best Actor (Bogart), Best Supporting Actor (Rains), Best Screenplay Adaptation, Best Editing, Best Score, and Best Cinematography. It won three: Best Picture, Best Director, and Best Screenplay Adaptation. But it should have won more.

There are a variety of explanations for this, but the simplest has its roots in Hollywood history: These things just happen. *Citizen Kane*, regarded as the greatest American film of all time, won one Academy Award for its screenplay. *Around the World in Eighty Days*, which will never be confused with a classic, won for Best Picture. Anyone who tries to use logic to figure out why the Academy Awards voting goes the way it does will soon require a straitjacket to help them in their calculations. In some years, there are few outstanding performances. In other years, there are dozens. In 1967, Rod Steiger won the Best Actor award for his redneck police chief in *In the Heat of the Night*. That meant that Paul Newman (*Cool Hand Luke*), Warren Beatty (*Bonnie and Clyde*), Dustin Hoffman (*The Graduate*), Spencer Tracy (*Guess Who's Coming to Dinner*) and Sidney Poitier (*In the Heat of the Night*) didn't win. You can't be reasonable about an unreasonable process.

Take, for instance, what happened to those parts of *Casablanca* which are regarded as legendary examples of movie making:

BOGART, who was nominated for Best Actor, lost to Paul Lukas in *Watch on the Rhine*. This was Lukas's only Oscar, and his performance as the family patriarch pursued by Nazi spies was superb. He would never be this good again. But better than Bogie? Let Lukas try and shoot someone

RICK: "I'M NOT INTERESTED IN POLITICS.
THE PROBLEMS OF THE WORLD ARE NOT IN MY
DEPARTMENT. I'M A SALOON-KEEPER."

with a .45 through the pocket of his raincoat and make it believable. Bogart got a measure of revenge in 1951, when he won for *The African Queen*—beating Marlon Brando for *A Streetcar Named Desire*.

RAINS. This was an even bigger miscarriage than passing over Bogart. Rains's performance—especially when he tells his subordinates to "round up the usual suspects" at the end of the film—is the stuff actors dream about. Rains was so good that his character made a 180-degree turn in personality, yet hardly anyone who sees the movie notices the incongruity in going from a corrupt, pandering cop to a war hero. Coburn, meanwhile, wasn't even the best part of *The More the Merrier;* Arthur was.

BERGMAN. *The Song of Bernadette* garnered twelve nominations in 1943; is there anyone today save for film buffs or former parochial school students who can remember what it was about? (A young Catholic girl who saw visions.) Jennifer Jones was a well-regarded actress who never won another Academy Award, although she did marry mogul David O. Selznick and co-starred with Bogart in the cult favorite, *Beat The Devil.* But she can't compare to Bergman. Watch Bergman in the scene during the flashback when Bogart suggests getting married on the train from Paris to Marseille. Why Bergman would be nominated for *For Whom the Bell Tolls* and not *Casablanca* is an even bigger mystery. Maybe it was the short haircut that did it.

THE SCORE. There are three generations of Americans who know the lyrics to "As Time Goes By." How many of today's filmgoers can name the Oscar winner for Best Score in 1943? (Alfred Newman for *The Song of Bernadette.*) Although composer Max Steiner may not have cared for "As Time Goes By," he didn't let it get in the way of his effort. Often, the best film music isn't noticed; Steiner's work is so good in *Casablanca* that it seems part of Rick's Café Américain. There are few musical moments in Hollywood history more riveting than the scene where the French nationals in the cafe sing the "Marseillaise," drowning out the German soldiers singing "Die Wacht am Rein."

Damning with Faint Praise /

Not everyone thinks *Casablanca* is the greatest movie ever made. In fact, there are quite a few respected critics who, like Julius Epstein, are thoroughly sick of the movie.

What a bunch of party poopers.

Still, they make several valid points. Some of the dialogue, as

Ingrid Bergman complained through the years, is hokey. Bergman's complaint is especially justified, since she got stuck with most of the clinkers: "Victor, please don't go to the Underground meeting tonight"; "Was that cannon fire? Or was it my heart pounding?"; and "Kiss me! Kiss me as though it was for the last time!"

Epstein particularly hated "A franc for your thoughts," another Bergman line that he says was written by Casey Robinson. And Curtiz does keep the camera moving so quickly that the weaknesses of the plot aren't noticeable; it seems perfectly natural to someone seeing the movie for the first time in 1972 (or 1982 or 1992) that Paul Henreid is wearing a white suit. Isn't that how everyone dressed in the olden days?

But these are quibbles, comparable to criticizing Shakespeare because he wasn't a college graduate (something critics would never do, would they?). The sum of the parts, in each case, is great enough to withstand any subtraction by any arbiters of taste and culture. Even the revisionist's revisionist, Andrew Sarris, says *Casablanca* is Curtiz's "one enduring masterpiece."

Nevertheless, in the interest of fairness (and because their comments almost always elicit a few chuckles), here's a look at what some of the movie's detractors have said through the years:

TIME, November 30, 1942: "Nothing short of an invasion could add much to *Casablanca*." This review, which wasn't signed, went on to pan Bogart, Greenstreet, Lorre, and Curtiz—and to reveal the ending.

THE NEW REPUBLIC, December 14, 1942: Manny Farber said the film "was as ineffectual as a Collier's short story." Collier's was a magazine that published slick, glossy, middle-of-the-road fiction. It has since gone out of business, which could also be said for Farber's opinion.

THE NEW STATESMAN, 1943: "Despite an exciting plot, the characters never walk out of their magazine covers. The love story that takes us from time to time into the past is horribly wooden, and clichés everywhere lower the tension."

PAULINE KAEL, in her 1968 book, *Kiss, Kiss, Bang, Bang*: "A movie that demonstrates how entertaining a bad movie can be. . . . One's tender sentiments will probably still be stirred, but in the cool night air afterward one may wonder a bit that this received the Academy Award as Best Picture for 1943."

Film theorist JOAN MELLEN, in her 1977 book, *Big Bad Wolves: Masculinity in the American Film*: A "crude exercise in political propaganda. . . ."

PETER HOUGE, *Film Comment*, May/June 1991: This piece is subtitled "A Heretical View of *Casablanca*," and Hogue runs down a six-point checklist that comes perilously close to examining the movie for political correctness. These problems, he writes, are "disturbing"—and the love story doesn't follow Henry James's criteria for romance.

Damning with Faint Praise II

Perhaps the only thing critics love to do more than to pan a picture is to try and explain it. It often seems as if they aren't happy unless they are dissecting camera angles in whichever current film is directed by whichever nouveau artiste is in style. Alfred Hitchcock, of course, suffers this fate all of the time. *The Birds*, for instance, has inspired all sorts of theses about his use of nature as an example of evil—while almost everyone overlooks the movie's lack of plot. No one has yet been able to explain why Suzanne Pleshette's character is in the movie, but there are a lot of explanations about how the birds symbolize everything from evil to eco-destruction.

As benefits a movie as steeped in myth, lore, and legend as *Casablanca*, there are plenty of theories as to what it really means. Of course, it would be too easy to take the film at face value—the story of a decent man in an indecent world who loses his bearings and then regains them—and to leave it at that. Just as critics have been jawing for hundreds of years about why Hamlet is the way he is (as if having his father murdered and his mother remarried shortly afterward wouldn't drive anyone crazy), they have concocted a variety of possibilities.

Here are some of the most common (and the least silly):

THE RICK BLAINE AS **FDR** THEORY: *Casa blanca* is Spanish for white house, and Franklin Delano Roosevelt was president in 1942. Laszlo, meanwhile, is Winston Churchill, urging Rick/FDR to give up his neutrality. This only makes sense to anyone willing to overlook the real reason Warners changed the title from *Everybody Comes to Rick's* to *Casablanca*—because *Algiers* had been a hit (both are cities in North Africa, for those who can't follow the intricacies of the Hollywood mind).

THE RICK BLAINE AS HOMOSEXUAL THEORY: This is a perennial critical favorite. It's hard to do any serious reading in American film or literature without discovering that someone, somewhere, says that a character, from Leatherstocking through Moby Dick to Jay Gatsby, is a repressed homosexual. It doesn't make any difference if, like Rick, they sleep around, or if, like Ernest Hemingway's Jake Barnes, they don't. In the former, say these critics, the men are trying too hard to prove their virility; in the latter, they have no interest because they don't like women. The evidence to support the Rick-as-homosexual theory comes from *Casablanca*'s ending: Not only do Rick and Renault walk

LOUIS AND RICK: A BEAUTIFUL FRIENDSHIP.

off together, but Renault has called him Ricky (a thoroughly gay term, say these critics). Of course, this theory doesn't take into consideration that it's possible for two men to be friends, but why quibble?

Film critic David Thomson supports this theory fictionally in *Suspects* (1985). (Yes, the book's title, and its epigraph, are borrowed from Renault's line.) ". . . Rick and Louis slipped off into the fog together. They went south, to Marrakech, and they lived there after the war. . . . Louis took the best care of him. . . ." The book is an entertaining collection of imagined life stories of movie characters from Marlene Dietrich in *Morocco* to Kathleen Turner in *Body Heat*, and the many cross-references are fascinating, especially for the true film fanatic.

THE RICK BLAINE AS OEDIPAL MAN THEORY: This is a doozy, as outlined by psychoanalyst Harvey Greenberg in his book, *The Movies on Your Mind*. Ilsa is the mother figure, Laszlo is the father figure, and Rick is going to kill his father figure and win the mother figure by withholding the letters of transit. Dr. Greenberg forgets, in his enthusiasm, that *Casablanca* is only a movie.

THE RICK BLAINE AS RHETT BUTLER THEORY: Rick Blaine/Rhett Butler, RB/RB . . . get it? This is one of the few that makes sense—up to a point. Sidney Rosenzweig, in his book about Michael Curtiz, points out that Rick and Rhett share the same Hollywood bloodlines: a mysterious background, a cynical shell hiding a sentimental nature, and a role as a sex symbol. On the other hand, one fights against fascism and the other fights for slavery, making an extended comparison increasingly irrelevant.

The Fundamental Things Apply
QUICK TAKES #4

♦ Humphrey Bogart wore a size-39 trenchcoat. Or so claimed the anonymous seller who wanted Christie's in New York City to auction a trenchcoat Bogart was supposed to have worn in *Casablanca*. The auction house estimated the coat would fetch between $15,000 and $20,000. However, the auction, scheduled for December 14, 1989, never took place. There were several doubts about the coat's authenticity, including a dispute about the brand. The coat to be auctioned was made by Ory-Kelly; however, studio records said Bogart's trenchcoats were made by Aquascutum.

◆ *Casablanca* did boffo business when it opened in 1942 and 1943, despite a severe winter in many parts of the country. The 1,500-seat Hollywood Theater sold 31,000 tickets in the first two weeks. One thing that helped were the reviews in the influential New York papers. Bosley Crowther in *The Times* said the movie "makes the spine tingle and the heart take a leap." Howard Barnes in the *Herald Tribune* called it "a smashing and moving melodrama." Take that, Manny Farber.

◆ Germany considered *Casablanca* a propaganda film, and it wasn't until after the war was over that it was allowed to play there. Even then, the censors took scissors to it and deleted twenty minutes from the film. All references to Nazis were cut, including every scene involving Conrad Veidt's Major Strasser.

◆ Even after *Casablanca* had been released and looked to be a hit, studio officials were unhappy with it—especially the ending. After U.S. President Franklin Roosevelt and British Prime Minister Winston Churchill held a summit meeting in the city in January 1943, Jack Warner wanted to reshoot the final scenes to include a reference to the summit meeting. Someone, thankfully, talked him out of it.

◆ That was almost as brilliant as the Warners marketing executive who insisted that the studio had to change the movie's name. It sounded, he said, too much like a brand of beer.

◆ Hal Wallis never forgot the pessimistic critiques his writers and producers gave *Casablanca*. He kept them in a file in his desk, and during story conferences forever after—whenever a writer or producer criticized his judgment—he would take out the *Casablanca* file. That, says, Wallis, always "ended all disagreements."

The End

#4

One of the many strengths of the studio system was that it offered studio executives an opportunity to get a variety of opinions about a proposal without having to leave the building. If a studio chief wanted to get a second opinion about whether to make a movie, he had dozens of well-read and intelligent people—writers, directors, and producers—at his immediate disposal. It was possible to send a writer a script, ask for a report on its viability, and get it by nine the next morning.

This was an invaluable tool for a man such as Hal Wallis, who knew how to use the opinions and advice other people gave him. In lesser hands, all of this information might paralyze the decision maker, and prove the theory that too much information is a dangerous thing. But Wallis was not that kind of mogul. The play, on his instructions, circulated around the Warners lot, and at least a dozen people read it, passed judgment, and wrote evaluations. As mentioned, almost all of them thought the play would make a crummy movie. One of them was Aeneas McKenzie, Wallis's first choice to write the screenplay. He was so daunted by the task ("Will require drastic revision . . . a tough job") that Wallis gave the Epsteins the picture.

Undoubtedly the most bizarre response came from Robert Lord, an associate producer who worked for Wallis. Wallis says he was extremely eager to get an opinion from Lord, whom he calls his favorite writer in his autobiography. But Lord's report couldn't have helped much.

He said the play was an obvious imitation of *Grand Hotel*, and that the characters seemed "very conventional and stereotyped." But he wasn't ready to give up on *Everybody Comes to Rick's* just because of that. No doubt Lord figured Wallis liked the play, so he decided to hedge his bet. There can be no other explanation for his subsequent suggestion.

Lord said Warners should put up money to produce *Everybody Comes to Rick's* as a play in exchange for the movie rights. Then, if the play was a hit, Warners had the makings of a hit movie. If the play flopped, then the studio was out only the money it put up, which would have been a fraction of what a flop movie would have cost to make.

Wallis does not comment on this in his book. Perhaps the report went into his *Casablanca* folder.

◆ Five ◆
The Imitators

$\mathcal{F}$ilm sequels and series are not a recent Hollywood phenomenon, no matter how many times in the past decade audiences have been forced to endure hordes of *Rocky*s, a plethora of *Police Academy*s, and a gaggle of *Friday the 13th*s.

In fact, they are a time-honored tradition, as much a part of movie lore as autocratic directors, hard-drinking actors, and sniveling agents. Where would film history be without *The Thin Man, After The Thin Man, Another Thin Man, Shadow of The Thin Man, The Thin Man Goes Home,* and *Song of The Thin Man*—the delightful screwball comedy/mysteries starring William Powell and Myrna Loy and based on the novel by Dashiell Hammett? And that's just one of the *good* ones. The Golden Era of Hollywood was filled with sequels and series as silly as anything Freddy Krueger ever dreamed up. How else to explain the dozen or so Ma and Pa Kettle movies, or the two Bonzo the chimp movies?

Then there is Hollywood's predilection for remakes, something almost as old as its fondness for sequels and series. Remakes are a second (or third or fourth or fifth) version of a previous movie. *The Front Page,* the quintessential newspaper play about an editor and his ace reporter (written by Ben Hecht and Charles MacArthur), was filmed in 1931; it was remade three times. That two of the remakes—1940's *His Girl Friday* with Cary Grant and Rosalind Russell and 1988's *Switching Channels* with Burt Reynolds and Kathleen Turner—changed the leads from two men to a man and a woman matters not a whit (nor does the move from the newsroom to the television studio in *Switching Channels*). In fact, another remake is 1952's *Last of the Comanches*—a Western that was first filmed as *Sahara*, a World War II Bogart picture.

Casablanca has been remarkably lucky, for it has avoided almost all of the pitfalls associated with remakes and sequels. According to a published study of Hollywood sequels, no one has had the nerve to try recapturing the movie's essence without the actors and script that made it what it was. Audiences have not been treated to *Return to Casablanca*, *Escape from Casablanca*, *One More Time in Casablanca* and *Play It Again, Casablanca*. Even the remakes failed to blemish the movie's memory, primarily because most starred Humphrey Bogart.

The movie generally acknowledged as a legitimate remake (although it was based on a lesser Hemingway novel of the same name) is Howard Hawks's 1945 film, *To Have and Have Not*, in which Bogart

TO HAVE AND HAVE NOT.

plays a man without convictions who is redeemed by his love for a good woman. Bogart plays a charter boat pilot who needs money and is talked into smuggling a couple of French Resistance leaders into Martinique. Hawks kept *Casablanca*'s World War II theme, but moved the locale from French North Africa to the French West Indies. He also changed the ending; Bogart gets the girl, who is played by Lauren Bacall. The Dooley Wilson part is played by Walter Brennan, who is Bogart's drunken hired hand. The Paul Henreid part is played by a woman, Dolores Moran, and the Conrad Veidt part is played by Dan Seymour (Abdul the doorman in *Casablanca*) as a Vichy police captain with a thick accent. This is a wisp of a movie, steeped in pseudo-atmosphere and redeemed only by Hawks's reputation as an auteur, some sharp dialogue by William Faulkner and Jules Furthman, and Bacall's mesmerizing screen debut. She is more than sultry; it's hard to understand why Bogart wastes his time dilly-dallying with Resistance leaders when he could be wooing Bacall. "You know how to whistle, don't you, Steve?" she tells him. "You just put your lips together and blow."

A better movie is *Key Largo*, which could be considered director John Huston's version of *Casablanca*. Made in 1948, it's based on the play of the same name by Maxwell Anderson, but its similarities to *Casablanca* are striking. Bogart plays a disillusioned World War II veteran visiting a dead buddy's widow (Bacall, in the Bergman part once again) and father (a wheelchair-bound Lionel Barrymore in the Henreid part). The hotel is taken over by a group of gangsters led by Edward G. Robinson (in the Conrad Veidt part), and in the course of the next couple of hours, Bogart again realizes there can be no compromise with evil. He shoots Robinson (in a nicely crafted scene on a small boat, where he also picks off Robinson's four henchmen), once again committing himself to the fight.

A disappointing "remake" is 1988's *Tequila Sunrise*, which billed itself as the "*Casablanca* of the '80s." It's a sloppy mess, with Mel Gibson and Kurt Russell in the Bogart and Henreid parts (although it's hard to tell which is which), Michelle Pfeiffer in the Bergman role, and Raul Julia hamming it up as the Rains character. It says a lot about this movie that Pfeiffer plays the owner of a chi-chi restaurant; only in Los Angeles would this be equated with fighting the Nazis.

A film with even more parallels to *Casablanca* was 1990's *Havana*.

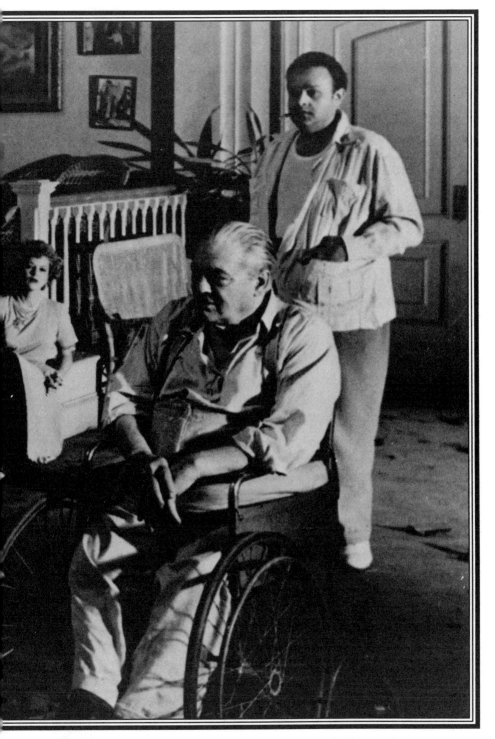

Key Largo.

MEL GIBSON, KURT RUSSELL, AND
MICHELLE PFEIFFER IN *TEQUILA SUNRISE.*

As directed by Sydney Pollack and written by Judith Rascoe and David
Rayfiel, the movie was an intentional *hommage* from the start. Robert
Redford plays a cynical American gambler recently arrived in Cuba
during the waning days of the corrupt Batista regime. It's not long
before he falls in love with a beautiful woman (Swedish actress Lena
Olin) who just happens to be married to an imprisoned upper-class
Communist (Raul Julia again) with ties to Fidel Castro. The ensuing
complications are played out against a background of smoke-filled
casinos and the war-torn countryside. An able supporting cast of good
actors (Alan Arkin, Tomas Milian, Mark Rydell) puts interesting spins on
various *Casablanca* roles, and there is some good dialogue, but the

ROBERT REDFORD AND LENA OLIN IN *HAVANA*.

movie never really comes together. The last scene, a poignant variation on that of the earlier film, only serves to point up the deficiencies of the previous two hours.

But a nadir of sorts was reached in 1980 with *Caboblanco*, directed by J. Lee Thompson. From the tinkling piano music in the first scene to the lookalike title, this is a blatant *Casablanca* pastiche—and a bad one. The post-WWII setting is a small fishing village on the coast of Peru controlled by ex-Nazi Jason Robards. Nightclub owner Charles Bronson is the tight-lipped American expatriate with a past, Dominique Sanda plays the mysterious French beauty looking for her Resistance lover, and Fernando Rey portrays the good/bad police captain with an eye for the ladies. The tired plot revolves around a fortune in ill-gotten jewels at the bottom of the ocean on a British ship. The film is badly written, directed, and acted; a scene involving Bronson, a German, and a petrol can is one of the silliest fights in screen history.

Sloppy is the kindest way to describe the only known proposed sequel to *Casablanca*. The 1943 plan, submitted to Warner Bros. by writer Frederick Stephani, is called *Brazzaville* (after Bogart's and Rains's destination at the end of *Casablanca*—"There's a Free French garrison over at Brazzaville," says Rains). That is the highlight of the treatment.

Stephani, who wrote the "Flash Gordon" serials for Universal in the late 1930s, apparently approached *Brazzaville* in the same way. "The material is eighty percent overboard," wrote Warners reader Frederick Faust (better known as Western author Max Brand and the creator of Dr. Kildare). It's hard to disagree with him. In the proposed sequel:

Rick Blaine is taken to the prefect's office after he shoots Major Strasser, where German officials insist Captain Renault arrest him. Renault stalls them because. . .

. . .The Allies are about to invade North Africa! And why does Renault know about the impending invasion? . . .

. . .Because he's an Allied counterspy! But that's okay, because Rick is an Allied agent, too. After everyone gets a chuckle out of this, Rick gets his next mission. He must go to Tangiers and infiltrate a German spy ring that is directing U-boat activity against Allied shipping. . .

. . .Where he opens a gambling club, using his cover from Casablanca! Then, Rick blackmails a U.S. consular official whose servant is part of the Nazi spy ring. This leads him to Maria, a dark and beautiful Nazi spy. . .

. . .Who falls in love with him! Meanwhile, Ilsa returns to Casablanca after Laszlo is killed. Then, despite Renault's warning, she goes to Tangiers to find Rick. . .

. . .In Maria's arms! Rick is torn between the two women, and he still hasn't penetrated the spy ring. But the Nazi master spy who heads the operation has seen through Rick, and plans a trap. . .

. . .Which Rick walks right into! Luckily for him, Maria throws herself in front of him, taking the bullet meant for Rick—at the same time Renault, who has followed Ilsa to Tangiers, shoots and kills the Nazi master spy. . .

. . .But before Rick and Ilsa can find "happiness at last," a dying Maria begs Rick to tell her that he loves her! Ilsa, crying, nods her approval, and Maria dies in Rick's arms.

Stephani, in his apparent haste to capitalize on the movie's success, overlooked the reasons for that success. Rick would no sooner be
a spy than he would put on a dress and sing love songs in his night club.
His entire character is based on a rejection of rules and the organiza-
tions that make them. Even his pre-Casablanca good deeds—running

"LIEB VATERLAND, MAGST RUHIG SEIN. . . ."

guns, fighting in Spain—are portrayed as the acts of a loner. And imagining Captain Renault as a double agent is even sillier. He spends more time seducing young girls than purloining German secret documents, to say nothing of bribe taking. It's possible to believe Renault could turn into a patriot; it's much harder to believe he could be a spy while he was torturing prisoners. The proposed sequel also overlooks the time reference in *Casablanca*, where it's December 1941. The Allied invasion of North Africa, meanwhile, didn't occur until November 1942 (which would make for a long wait in the prefect's office for Rick and Renault). And what's Stephani doing calling his sequel *Brazzaville* when it takes place in Tangiers?

You Must Remember This

TRIVIA INTERLUDE #5

MAJOR STRASSER WEARS A:

____ carnation
____ flowered necktie
____ monacle
____ beret

Carnation (probably to make him as dapper as Victor Laszlo).

WHEN RICK JOINS MAJOR STRASSER AT HIS TABLE, THE MAJOR IS EATING:

____ chips and picante sauce
____ caviar
____ popcorn
____ nuts

Caviar.

WHAT ARE THE NAMES OF ALLAN FELIX'S FRIENDS IN
***PLAY IT AGAIN, SAM*, AND WHO PLAYED THEM?**

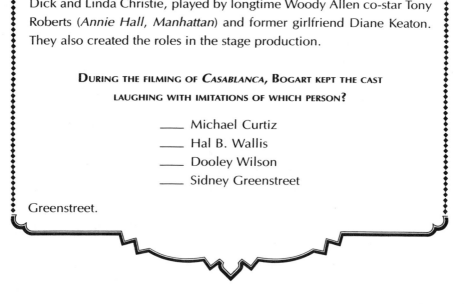

Dick and Linda Christie, played by longtime Woody Allen co-star Tony Roberts (*Annie Hall*, *Manhattan*) and former girlfriend Diane Keaton. They also created the roles in the stage production.

DURING THE FILMING OF *CASABLANCA*, BOGART KEPT THE CAST LAUGHING WITH IMITATIONS OF WHICH PERSON?

____ Michael Curtiz
____ Hal B. Wallis
____ Dooley Wilson
____ Sidney Greenstreet

Greenstreet.

Who's Who in Casablanca

THE IMITATORS

Anyone who doubts that *Casablanca* has become part of American culture need look no further than the card catalog of their local library, where they will find any number of books entitled *As Time Goes By* (one of which is a study of pop music in the 1960s). There is a ceiling fan company named after *Casablanca*, as well as bars and restaurants throughout the country called things like "Rick's Place." The movies, too, are full of references—both reverential and not—to the film, from the Peter Falk sendup in *The Cheap Detective* to Albert Finney's paean to Bogart in *Gumshoe*. On television, *Casablanca* spoofs have been a staple of variety shows as well as situation comedies (including the predominantly black *227*). It would be a hopeless task to track down and relate every incident, but the best-known is Woody Allen's play and film, *Play It Again, Sam*.

Musicians, too, are not immune to the bug, no matter how much more hip than everyone they pretend to be. It would be impossible to detail all of the musically related developments of the past fifty years, but several are worth noting. There was a French-Canadian band in the late 1980s called Bogart, while an English New Wave band had a minor FM hit in 1981 with a film-noirish song called "Playing Bogart": "If you lose when playing Bogart," went the chorus, "you're better on your own/Sit on my bed and smoke a single cigarette in the dark." And who can forget the wonderfully horrible "Key Largo," Bertie Higgins's love song that reached #8 on the Billboard pop charts in 1982? Its chorus— "We had it all, just like Bogey and Bacall. . . . Here's looking at you, kid. . . ."—ignores completely that Bogart spoke those words to Ingrid Bergman, and not Lauren Bacall, his co-star in *Key Largo*.

But fidelity to language has never been an important part of the *Casablanca* legend—ironic given how important language is to the movie's success. As noted, there are dozens of memorable speeches, yet the best-known is never spoken by any of the characters. "Play it again, Sam" has become an immortal line in the history of the American cinema, as well as the title of Allen's stage and film tributes to the Bogart persona. But all Bergman says is "Play it once, Sam, for old time's sake" while the closest Bogart comes is "You played it for her, you can play it for me. . . . If she can stand it, I can. Play it!"

Don't spend too much time wondering how that transformation happened. It's almost impossible to pin down, and such misquotations aren't unique to the movies. It's like the old children's game of Telephone; once a phrase enters popular use, its origins are obscure. American culture is full of supposed sayings, from William Tecumseh Sherman's "War is Hell" (Bartlett claims Robert E. Lee said it, and in a different context) to Knute Rockne's "Win one for the Gipper" (which probably didn't happen). "I know [Bogart] never actually said, 'Play it again, Sam,' but I said it enough for both of us," Allen told *Life* magazine in 1969.

Allen's 1969 play, which Herbert Ross directed in 1972 as a film, hasn't aged especially well. But it still holds up better than something like *To Have and Have Not*. Allen plays Allan Felix, a film critic whose wife leaves him and who then strikes out with a variety of women, including a nymphomaniac and an aspiring actress who appeared in a porn movie. For advice, he turns to the spirit of Humphrey Bogart, whom he desperately wants to be like. Bogart, after all, could get any woman he desired, and he would do it in a suave and sophisticated manner. Allan, on the other hand, can only be described as a bumbling fool. Bogart impersonator Jerry Lacy played the role in the stage and

**WOODY ALLEN AND THE GHOST OF
RICK IN _PLAY IT AGAIN, SAM._**

film versions as Dear Abby in a trenchcoat and fedora—"Women need a slap . . . . All you gotta do is whistle."

Both play and movie end with a climactic airport scene that copies the airport scene in _Casablanca_ (and the movie includes a propeller-driven airplane shot at the same angles as in the original). Allan renounces his girlfriend—who also happens to be his best friend's wife—using much the same speech Rick uses to send Ilsa off with

Laszlo. Better yet, when the girlfriend compliments him on being so noble and understanding, Allan says, "That's from *Casablanca*. I've been waiting all of my life to say that." Although Allen adapted the movie from his play, much of the credit for the movie's *Casablanca*-style scenes is given to Ross. The director decided to open the movie with Allan, in a theater, watching the airport scene in *Casablanca*. This reinforces the *Casablanca* parallel throughout much of the rest of the film. The play, on the other hand, opens with Allan, in front of a television, watching the final scene in *The Maltese Falcon*, where Bogart turns Mary Astor over to the police. This gives the play more of a Bogart theme than a *Casablanca* theme. Ross also added *Casablanca's* Bergman-Bogart kiss, which is cut into the scene where Allan kisses his girlfriend for the first time, reinforcing the parallel.

Still, the lesson from both play and movie comes from *Casablanca*. Rick, the loner, can't act for anyone but himself, and he can't let anyone else prevent him from doing what he thinks is right. Says Allan to the Bogart character: "The secret's not being you, it's being me. True, you're not too tall and kinda ugly. But I'm short enough and ugly enough to succeed by myself."

But the Sets Don't Match

Producer David L. Wolper had courage. Not only did he want to make a weekly television series modeled on *Casablanca*, but he wanted to do it with actor David Soul in the Humphrey Bogart part.

Soul's previous claim to fame was as one of the leads in *Starsky and Hutch*, a telling example of how bad television can be. Soul and co-star Paul Michael Glaser played tough-talking, tough-dressing, and tough-driving cops who singlehandedly—while ignoring all attempts by their bosses to restrain them—cleaned up their city every week in the mid-1970s.

This was not the first time television had tried its hand at reproducing *Casablanca*. In 1955, a "Casablanca" segment was one-third of *Warner Brother Presents*, an hour-long series on ABC hosted by Gig Young. This TV "Casablanca" debuted on September 13 and starred raspy-voiced Charles McGraw as Rick Jason, with several of the Warners stock company in supporting roles: Marcel Dalio (the croupier in

CHARLES McGRAW.

the movie) as Renault and Dan Seymour (Abdul the doorman in the movie) as Ferrari. This "Casablanca" alternated with serial adaptations of the films *Cheyenne* and *Kings Row*. *Warner Brothers Presents* lasted one season, and the "Casablanca" portion aired eleven or so episodes. When it went off the air, few people noticed. Its last episode was April 24, 1956.

But Wolper in 1982 had different plans, even though Soul's selection caused more than a few TV critics to wonder if Wolper was beaten before he started. Still, he had impressive credentials. Wolper's company had produced the 1964 Bogart documentary, *A Man Called Bogart*, he was a long-time veteran of the weekly television grind, and he had permission from Warner Bros. to use the movie's original sets.

"I liked the clear morality of 1941, when you had no doubt about good and evil," Wolper told *The New York Times* in 1983, shortly before the program debuted on NBC. "There was a lot of idealism, people fighting for a cause. People are searching for morality today."

They did not, however, search very hard for the television "Casablanca." It aired for just five weeks: three in April (premiering April 10, 1983), and two more episodes at the end of August and the beginning of September to fill time on the schedule before the 1984 season began. NBC didn't order any more programs after it used the original five.

The series failed in the ratings despite an adequate cast—Ray Liotta was Sacha the bartender, Hector Elizondo was Captain Renault, and Scatman Crothers played Sam—and some fairly intelligent scripts. The scripts placed the television show in the June 1940 to November 1941

DAVID SOUL, RAY LIOTTA, AND HECTOR ELIZONDO
IN THE **1983 TV** SHOW.

period, after Rick arrives from France but before Ilsa and Laszlo come to Casablanca.

But even *People* magazine, not known for hard-hitting critiques, panned the show. Typical was the review in *The New York Times*: "There seems to be some confusion whether it is supposed to be doing homage or parody. It ends up nowhere."

In fact, much of the atmosphere in the episodes was strained. It seemed as if everyone was waiting around for Bogart to show up and say, "OK, enough of this nonsense. Let's get a drink."

The series was not helped by Soul's personal problems. Although Bogart had been able to use his marital struggles with Mayo Methot to strengthen his performance, Soul wasn't as fortunate (or as skilled as an actor). In October 1982, after production had started on the series, he was arrested for hitting his wife. Their marriage had been floundering for several months, and Soul had been drinking heavily for some time before that.

SCATMAN CROTHERS AT THE PIANO
IN RICK'S CAFÉ AMÉRICAIN.

The Sets Still Don't Match

Murray Burnett has never given up trying to get *Everybody Comes to Rick's* produced on the stage. His most recent attempt came in 1991, when, at the age of eighty, he rewrote his original three-act play into a two-act drama called *Rick's Bar Casablanca*. The only stage productions of *Casablanca* in the past fifty years were based on the movie, and not Burnett's play.

His time, said London critics and audiences, could have been much better spent.

The new play, based on the first, never-produced play and the movie, opened at the Whitehall Theater in London on April 10 and closed May 11. It starred Britisher Leslie Grantham as Rick Blaine, American Shelley Thompson as Lois Meredith (the Ilsa Lund character before the Epstein brothers changed her name and nationality), and Trevor Michael Georges as Sam.

The play cost almost half a million dollars (two-thirds of what the movie cost), and was staged with Warner Bros.' permission. The goal was to turn a successful London run into a box-office bonanza on Broadway in time for the film's fiftieth anniversary, tying in the studio's interests with those of Burnett and producers Paul Elliott and Greg Smith.

But *Rick's Bar Casablanca* never got that far—apparently on its merit. Wrote *Variety*: "The theme of *Casablanca* is worthy and timeless. The same can't be said of this play."

The Sets Still Don't Match (and They're the Wrong Color)

Someone, somewhere must enjoy the colorized version of *Casablanca*. It's hard to believe that Turner Entertainment, which owns the rights to the movie, would have spent untold thousands of dollars to colorize it in 1988 if no one had wanted to watch it.

Not that anyone should want to watch it.

Regardless of the merits of colorization, a highly controversial process that has inflamed passions in Hollywood since the mid-1980s, it's hard to see why Turner colorized *Casablanca*. If Warner Bros. had wanted to make a color version in 1942, they could have. Color films were not unusual, and several of the studio's biggest hits had been in color—among them *The Adventures of Robin Hood* in 1938, directed in part by *Casablanca*'s Michael Curtiz. *Gone With the Wind* made a big splash a year later with its color. Critic Roger Ebert has pointed out that the studios consciously chose to make films like *Casablanca*—that relied on clever dialogue instead of action to advance the plot—in black and white. That way, the reasoning went, the audience paid more attention to the actors than to the scenery.

The biggest objection to colorization, though, is that it doesn't look very good. The process is still comparatively primitive, and involves a computer painting each scene according to a preset program. The best analogy is that the computer paints each scene by number, in much the same way a small child paints a scene of a sailboat by number. This limits the palette, since it would be nearly impossible to program the computer for every shading and nuance that exists in the real world. Instead, the program limits the computer to a number of basic colors— one kind of blue, one kind of green, one kind of brown, and so on.

This makes for a certain sameness. Every yellow in the colorized version of *Casablanca*, for example, is the same, whether it's Dooley Wilson's mustard-yellow dinner jacket or a yellow flower. And some of the colors don't match what they are known to be. The water in the Seine River in the Paris flashback scene is green, and Victor Laszlo's infamous white suit is a sort of beige. And it doesn't help that all of the Anglos in the movie look as if they just stepped out of a tanning salon.

The Fundamental Things Apply
QUICK TAKES #5

◆ That blue dress that Ilsa puts away when the Germans marched into Paris wasn't a dress at all. When Turner's employees colorized the movie, they discovered something no one else had ever seen: Ilsa was wearing a pinstriped suit and a white blouse. The Warners' wardrobe department goofed, and hadn't put her in a dress. "I never noticed that,

RICK: "Louis, I wouldn't like to shoot you, but I will if you take one more step."

RENAULT: "UNDER THE CIRCUMSTANCES, I WILL SIT DOWN."

and I've seen the film many times," Turner Entertainment president Roger Mayer told the *Los Angeles Times*. "I don't think many people would."

♦ In 1987, for a private showing at Brazil's Rio Film Festival, Joao Luis Albuquerque re-edited a print of *Casablanca* and changed the ending—Bergman doesn't get on the plane, but comes back into Bogart's arms.

♦ When David Wolper arranged with Warners Bros. to use the original plans and sets for his 1983 television *Casablanca*, he discovered that there was not just one set, but three. Rick's Café Américain was built in three parts, which had helped make it easier to film. He also was surprised to find that the parts didn't fit together, since they were constructed as separate pieces. Wolper was only able to use the movie's bar and its doors. The sets are apparently still standing on some Warners back lot in Burbank.

♦ Projectionist P.M. Summer thought it was a terrific idea, although the management of the Dobie Theater in Austin, Texas, wasn't as amused with his scheme one day in 1973. Summer spliced the end of *Casablanca* into the beginning of *Play It Again, Sam*, turning the separate features into one seamless, four-hour film. But the theater's management, faced with the loss of concessions because of the missing intermission, told him never to do it again.

♦ Although no one has had the nerve to film another version of *Casablanca*, the producers of the "Lux Radio Theater" had no such doubts about their medium. They offered a condensed, revised version of the movie in 1943 starring Alan Ladd and Hedy Lamarr (who finally got an opportunity to play Ilsa). Lamarr is okay, Ladd is barely adequate (Raymond Chandler once described him as a child's version of a tough guy) and John Loder, stuck with playing Captain Renault, isn't even that. To make matters worse, the radio broadcast doesn't use the movie's dialogue verbatim. This is not unlike signing Joe DiMaggio for your baseball team and then not playing him in every game because you are afraid the fans will be bored with perfection.

♦ Woody Allen, of course, is not the only director influenced by *Casablanca* and the Bogart persona. François Truffaut, as mentioned, made use of those themes. So did no less a seminal figure in the development of the cinema than Jean-Luc Godard. Godard, a critic and filmmaker, made *Breathless* in 1959 and launched the New Wave, which redefined the role of movies in popular culture. And in *Breathless* (written by Truffaut), a T-shirted Jean-Paul Belmondo (described by one critic as looking more like a boxer than a movie star) divides his time between fleeing from the police and posing in front of a Bogart poster, mouthing "Bo-gie."

The End

5

Casablanca, Gone With the Wind, and *Citizen Kane* are generally considered to be the three best-known movies in Hollywood history.

This does not mean, however, that anyone in Hollywood knows anything about *Casablanca*.

In 1982, writer Chuck Ross submitted the screenplay of *Casablanca* to 217 movie agents. Ross sent them the script verbatim, save for the title, which he changed to *Everybody Comes to Rick's*, and the name of Dooley Wilson's character, which he changed from Sam to Dooley. Ross also used a pseudonym, Erik Demos (*demos* is Greek for "the common man").

The results were astounding, even to someone as cynical as Ross. (He had performed a similar experiment on book publishers several years earlier. In that case, fifteen out of fifteen had rejected a book that had not only been published, but had won a National Book Award. One of those fifteen had published the original book.)

Of the 217 agents (selected from a list screened by the Writers Guild of America), ninety returned the screenplay unread because they did not review unsolicited manuscripts and forty-two manuscripts were either lost in the mail or lost in the mailroom at an agency.

Of the remaining eighty-five, only thirty-three recognized the script—or approximately one in three. It's mind-boggling to think that two out of every three agents in Hollywood wouldn't recognize *Casablanca* (which probably goes a long way toward explaining why Hollywood makes the movies it does). That percentage drops to about one out of six by including the ninety agencies that didn't read unsolicited manuscripts. Looked at that way, only one out of six Guild-screened agencies would not turn down a chance to represent *Casablanca* today; which, incidentally, is less than the chance of winning on the first throw at craps.

Among the highlights of Ross's test, which appeared in the November/December 1982 issue of *Film Comment*:

Three agencies offered to represent the script, and one said it had submitted it to a studio.

Another agency said it wasn't sure it would make a good movie, but wanted to recommend a literary agent in New York to see if the screenplay could be sold as a novel.

Eight agencies thought the script resembled *Casablanca*. Said one: "I don't know if it was my imagination or not, but I found it somewhat like *Casablanca*. I thought the beginning was almost exactly like it." What about the rest of it? asked Ross. "Well, no, then it departed more."

The remaining replies were mixed, but all were familiar to anyone who has ever submitted material to an agent, publisher, or studio. One man told Ross to read a popular screenwriting textbook, since the dialogue in his submission needed polish. Several others said the plot was dull, the storyline was uninteresting, and that the characters were unappealing.

The best reply came from the Ray Rappa Agency, and it was nothing if not honest: "It's a good script, but in this business it's more the deal and what you've got cooking packagewise. It's not an easy row to hoe when you take a new script and a new writer."

Richard Corliss, the magazine's longtime editor, put the Ross experiment into perspective: "They don't make movies like *Casablanca* any more," he wrote. "And all things considered, it's no wonder."

*A*nyone can like *Casablanca*, and millions do. Almost anyone can be a *Casablanca* fan, and that the movie remains popular fifty years after its release proves that.

But what does it take to be a Casablanquiste? Is it enough to know the difference between the General De Gaulle and the General Weygand letters of transit? Is it sufficient to own the scene-by-scene photo screenplay, or is ownership of the record album featuring the soundtrack music required?

Actually, all it takes is the ability to watch Rick Blaine drink himself into a stupor and understand—completely, passionately, and in-stantly—exactly how he feels. The other stuff is window dressing.

But the other stuff is also a lot of fun, and it's necessary to convert others to the cause. They can't believe in Rick Blaine unless they watch him wave his bourbon bottle around first. The basic *Casablanca* library should include:

THE VIDEO TAPE (Turner Entertainment)—and in black and white, not color. The video is available at almost every video store in the country, and through just about every mail order distributor. If it's unavailable locally, try RKO Video (800/942-4144).

THE POSTER. Reproductions of the eight original posters (not including smaller lobby cards) start at less than $10, and they are available at a variety of retail outlets across the country. In fact, there is a Yellow Pages entry for "Movie Posters" in the phone book. Originals, by the way, are priced according to demand, and are quite the collector's item. Prices range from $3,000 for a 14"x22" poster to more than $12,000 for the largest, 22"x28", poster.

THE BOOK. *Casablanca* (Universal, 1974), edited by Richard J. Anobile, offers the movie in frame-by-frame sequence, with the dialogue for each scene accompanying each frame. There is also an interview with Ingrid Bergman. Unfortunately, this book is out of print, and its publisher has no plans to reissue it for the fiftieth anniversary of the film's release. However, a variety of mail-order companies and used-book stores specialize in hard-to-find books and in remainders—books that aren't printed anymore, but may still be sitting in boxes in a warehouse. Check the "Book dealers, used and rare" section of the Yellow Pages. Also a good source: New York City's Strand Bookstore (212/473-1452), one of the country's best used bookstores.

THE DOCUMENTARIES. Two are essential—*Bacall on Bogart* (Turner Entertainment, 1988) and *Ingrid* (HBO Studio Productions, 1987). Both are informative, revealing, and don't make the mistake of unduly gushing over their subjects. The former first appeared as part of the PBS *Great Performances* series in 1988, and it has that PBS polish. Lauren Bacall narrates the ninety-minute program, which includes rare footage of some of Bogart's worst film moments, such as his turn as a zombie in *The Return of Dr. X.* Also appearing is Julius J. Epstein, who discusses the production of *Casablanca* (in apparently his only film interview on the subject), and a little-seen clip of Ingrid Bergman (apparently from a rare BBC documentary about Bogart). *Ingrid*, shown as part of Cinemax's "Crazy About the Movies" series, offers its share of little- and previously seen footage: home movies of Bergman as a child, shot by her father; scenes from several of her first Swedish films; and candid discussions by her co-stars (Anthony Quinn among them) about her ability as an actor. Also worth looking for, although not available on video, is the 1963 documentary, *A Man Called Bogart.* It has been sold to syndication, and still turns up occasionally late at night on television, interspersed between vocational training commercials, get-rich-quick seminars, and ads for 1-900 sex lines.

THE REFERENCES. *The Complete Films of Humphrey Bogart* (Carol, 1990) and *The Films of Ingrid Bergman* (Citadel, 1970). Each book contains stills from each actor's films (although the Bergman book doesn't include her final four movies). There are also synopses of each film, cast lists, and biographical essays on each star. The Bogart essay, by Clifford McCarty, is especially worthwhile, since Bogart never wrote an auto-biography and the existing books about him are woefully incomplete. The Bergman book includes reviews of each of the films by contemporary critics, offering Casablanquistes a chance to see the infamous 1943 James Agee notice in *The Nation*: "Obviously an improvement on one of the world's worst plays. . . ." There are several of these types of books for each actor, but these two volumes seem to be the most thorough.

THE VIDEODISC. *Casablanca* (The Criterion Collection, 1989) is almost worth owning even for people who don't have anything to play it on. The liner notes by film historian Ronald Haver (who helped produce the disc) include such crucial minutae as Michael Curtiz's acceptance speech on winning the Best Director Oscar ("Always a bridesmaid, never a mother") as well as a cast list complete to forty-two speaking parts, and the credits for each of the eleven songs in the movie. Anyone who does have access to a videodisc player will be overwhelmed. The disc not only has a gloriously vivid black-and-white version of the film, but a revealing commentary by Haver on an audio overtrack detailing the film's history. There is newsreel footage of the city of Casablanca in 1943 when Roosevelt and Churchill held their conference, excerpts from the Lux radio broadcast, production and budget notes, the theatrical trailer and publicity stills (including Bogart making home movies of the filming), a comparison of the black-and-white and colorized versions and the infamous proposed sequel. The videodisc is available at retail outlets throughout the country as well as by mail from the distributor, Voyager (213/451-1383).

THE RECORD. *Casablanca: Classic Film Scores for Humphrey Bogart* (RCA Red Seal, 1974) is out of print, but it isn't hard to find in used record stores. In fact, it has become something of a collector's item, with the original $6 album selling for as much as $15. The album features four pages of liner notes by Rudy Behlmer, the movie's other leading historian, as well as excerpts from the musical soundtracks for twelve Bogart movies. More than eight minutes are devoted to *Casablanca*, including orchestral and piano versions of "As Time Goes By."

You Must Remember This

TRIVIA INTERLUDE #6

WHERE WAS LASZLO HIDING WHEN ILSA LEFT RICK WAITING AT THE RAILROAD STATION IN PARIS?

In a freight car on the outskirts of town.

MATCH THE CHARACTERS WITH THE HATS THEY WEAR IN THE MOVIE:

1. Renault   a. fedora
2. Rick   b. Panama
3. Laszlo   c. kepi
4. Ferrari   d. fez
5. Abdul   e. officer's cap
6. Strasser   f. pith helmet

Renault/kepi; Rick/fedora; Laszlo/Panama; Ferrari/pith helmet; Abdul/fez; Strasser/officer's cap.

WHY DOES RENAULT CLOSE THE CAFE AFTER MAJOR STRASSER TELLS HIM IT WOULD BE A GOOD IDEA (FOLLOWING THE "MARSEILLAISE" SCENE)?

He closes it because he's "shocked to find that gambling is going on here!" —just before the croupier hands him his gambling winnings.

"AS TIME GOES BY" IS THE BEST-KNOWN SONG IN *CASABLANCA*, BUT IT ISN'T, AS MENTIONED, ORIGINAL TO THE MOVIE. HOWEVER, ONE SONG WAS WRITTEN ESPECIALLY FOR THE MOVIE, AND HAS BECOME A STANDARD. WHAT'S THE SONG?

"Knock on Wood," written by M.K. Jerome and Jack Scholl.

WHAT COLOR ARE RICK'S EYES?

____ Brown

____ Green

____ Blue

____ Black

Brown. "Are my eyes really brown?" he asks Major Strasser when the Nazi hands him a copy of his dossier.

Who's Who in Casablanca

THE SOURCES

Movie stars—and the producers and directors who work with them—have big egos. This seems to be a requirement for the job; after all, it takes a tremendous amount of self-confidence to stand in front of a camera and cry or scream or make love to a stranger.

But careers end, while egos don't. This presents a problem, and its solution has turned into quite a windfall for anyone interested in pursuing the truth behind the making of *Casablanca*. One of the easiest ways to maintain an ego is to write a book, and there are thousands of biographies and autobiographies written by Hollywood's notables (and less-than-notables)—including a number by or about the principals in *Casablanca*.

This makes it possible for anyone to research the movie and its history and legend without having to spend long, dusty hours at the Warner Bros. archives at the University of Southern California in Los Angeles. One of the best places to start, in fact, is a book expressly written from these biographic and autobiographic sources—Otto Friedrich's *City of Nets* (Harper & Row, 1986). Friedrich, working with a vow of "no more interviews," has put together a compelling history of the movies in the 1940s, which covers the period from the height of the studio system to its collapse. He especially loves to show how the same story—say, the time William Faulkner was told he could work at home

RENAULT: "MAJOR STRASSER'S BEEN SHOT.
ROUND UP THE USUAL SUSPECTS."

and so returned to Mississippi—is claimed by several people. Friedrich successfully synthesizes hundreds of books and interviews about Hollywood in the forties to provide about as accurate a portrait as is possible for an industry built on imagination.

One general reference even more valuable is *The Encyclopedia of Film* (Putnam, 1991). Its entries, organized alphabetically and covering actors, directors, producers, writers, and technicians, include biographical information and the complete filmography of each performer. It is here that Humphrey Bogart's actual birth date is listed, and not the fiction of Christmas Day, 1899 (which even Lauren Bacall insists is true). It's also handy to have a book like Leonard Maltin's *TV Movies and Video Guide*. The volume, updated annually, contains casts, ratings, and plots for almost 20,000 movies.

The three standard references for the movie itself are the "*Casa-*

blanca" chapter in Rudy Behlmer's *Behind the Scenes* (Samuel French, 1990), Ronald Haver's "Finally, the Truth about *Casablanca"* in the June 1976 issue of *American Film* magazine, and Charles Francisco's "You Must Remember This. . . . The Filming of *Casablanca"* (Prentice-Hall, 1980). The Behlmer book, which includes a copy of the Warners reader's report synopsis of *Everybody Comes to Rick's*, is scholarly and accurate without being dull or pretentious. The only drawback is that the production and filming chronology is muddled; several dates don't seem to match. The Haver article, and companion letters in the October 1976 issue of *American Film*, is one of the first attempts—and one of the best—to settle the issue of who wrote the screenplay. Haver, the longtime director of film programs at the Los Angeles County Museum of Art and the author of *David O. Selznick's Hollywood*, is the undisputed authority on *Casablanca*. Anything he writes about the movie is worth reading. The Francisco book is out of print and very difficult to find (its publisher has been sold), but is worth the effort. Francisco, who has also written a number of Hollywood biographies, did his homework and seems well-informed. Perhaps his book will be reissued to coincide with the movie's fiftieth anniversary.

Humphrey Bogart may have been the biggest star in Hollywood for a decade during his life and one of the biggest stars ever since his death, but a satisfactory biography has yet to be written (and he died before he could write an autobiography). "No one [has] done justice to the man yet," Bacall wrote in her book, *By Myself* (Knopf, 1978), which is more than satisfactory. Unfortunately for Casablanquistes, it touches only briefly on the movie. The best of a bad lot of the Bogart biographies is Nathaniel Benchley's *Humphrey Bogart* (Little, Brown, 1975). Benchley, son of humorist Robert Benchley, friend to both Bogart and Bacall, and a respected writer himself, can't stop fawning over his subject no matter how hard he tries. An interesting, if different, effort is Ezra Goodman's *The Good Bad Guy* (Lyle Stuart, 1965). Goodman, a former newspaperman and studio publicity hack, couldn't stand Bogart, and he spends 223 pages telling why. Journalist Joe Hyams has written two Bogart books, and it's enough to say that Bacall was correct when she wrote that her introduction to the first one was better than the book. There are countless other Bogie books, and most follow the lead of the one that claims to be "a candid, authoritative portrait of the remarkable man who has become an existential symbol to a whole generation." A better bet is to find a copy of the Peter Bogdanovich essay about Bogart in the September 1964 issue of *Esquire*.

There are no such problems with learning about Ingrid Bergman's life. She has acquired not only a notable biographer (Laurence Leamer), but left an honest and accurate autobiography, *My Story* (Delacorte, 1980). Bergman's autobiography is a combination of letters and diary entries printed verbatim, interspersed with Bergman's recollections and historical material written by collaborator Alan Burgess. The Leamer book, *As Time Goes By: The Life of Ingrid Bergman* (Harper & Row, 1986), is professional, thorough, and competent. Maybe he can be convinced to do the same thing for Bogart. Neither book spares the star's feelings; Bergman is especially candid about the men in her life, from her husbands to her boyfriends to her leading men.

Interestingly, the only principal member of the production without a book is Claude Rains. Hal B. Wallis (*Starmaker*, MacMillan, 1980) and Paul Henreid (*Ladies' Man*, St. Martin's, 1984) have autobiographies; both books offer useful information about the movie and plenty of gossip (especially about Michael Curtiz's sexual escapades). Both men also have a few scores to settle, and allowances for the truth should be made in these instances. It's amazing how each of them remembered the smallest slight, especially if it was committed by Warners contract director Irving Rapper.

Peter Lorre and Sidney Greenstreet appear together, not surprisingly, in Ted Sennett's *Masters of Menace* (E.P. Dutton, 1979). Sennett goes into great detail about each man's life and career, making this the best place to learn about all of the "B" movies the duo made. Sennett also provides information about the Epstein brothers' role in *Casablanca* that is unavailable elsewhere. There is no Curtiz autobiography, but an academic, yet readable, study of his films exists: Sidney Rosenzweig's *Casablanca and Other Major Films of Michael Curtiz* (UMI Research Press, 1982). It's not only an appreciation of Curtiz's efforts on *Casablanca*, but an attempt to elevate him into the ranks of the auteur directors. Also recommended is Barry Paris's article in the December 1990 *American Film*, "The Little Tyrant Who Could."

One of the reasons Howard Koch seemed to get most of the credit for writing *Casablanca* over the past twenty years is that he wrote two books and the Epsteins didn't write any. Yet today, it's hard to see why either of Koch's accounts made that much of a difference. In the first,

"WE'LL ALWAYS HAVE PARIS."

Casablanca: Script and Legend (Overlook Press, 1973), he takes the lion's share of the credit; in the second, *As Times Go By: Memoirs of a Writer* (Harcourt Brace Jovanovich, 1979), he is much more circumspect. In either case, both books are restrained versions of history; the former's script, for instance, is nothing more than the dialogue of the completed movie transcribed on paper. This discretion is an astonishing development: After all, the second book is an autobiography that

143

includes details of Koch's blacklisting (though to be sure, there is something commendable in Koch's refusal to criticize his accusers). The best source for the Epsteins' side of the story is in *Backstory* (University of California, 1986), a collection of interviews with screenwriters of the thirties, forties, and fifties. Julius Epstein has also done numerous magazine and archival interviews in the past decade to stake he and his brother's claim to the script. One of the most entertaining is with Maurice Zolotow in the September 1988 issue of *Los Angeles* magazine. *Backstory* also has a condensed version of the Casey Robinson interview where he takes credit for the screenplay. A thoughtful, realistic overview of the gilded cage of the Hollywood writer is Ian Hamilton's *Writers in Hollywood* (HarperCollins, 1990). Hamilton, who learned about surrealism when he tried to write J.D. Salinger's unauthorized biography, put the entire screenplay controversy in perspective: "Howard Koch was happy enough to be remembered as the man who wrote *Casablanca*: After all, the alternative was to be remembered as the man who wrote *Mission to Moscow*."

The Fundamental Things Apply
QUICK TAKES #6

♦ Here's why it's hard to believe anything in Hollywood biographies. In his book, Hal Wallis says Vincent Sherman, a Warners contract director, didn't seem excited about directing *Casablanca*, and so wasn't considered for the job. Sherman, on the other hand, said that he was one of the few people at Warners who liked the play *Everybody Comes to Rick's*. He was, he said, the man who piqued the Epsteins' interest in writing the script after describing the play to them. And, said Sherman, he was hurt when Curtiz got the directing assignment.

♦ Jack Warner's relationship with Wallis had deteriorated so badly by the early 1940s that he once sent Wallis a telegram blasting him for taking all of the credit for the studio's successes. He threatened to sue Wallis if the practice continued, ignorant of newspaper practices that prevented Wallis from having any control over what finally ended up in print.

♦ Figure this one: The photograph on the cover of Wallis's book is from *Casablanca*. The photograph on the cover of a book called, *Hollywood in the Forties* is from *Casablanca*. The photograph on the cover of one of Joe Hyams's biographies is from *Casablanca*. But the photo on the cover of *The Complete Films of Humphrey Bogart* is a studio publicity shot of Bogart wearing a sport shirt.

◆ If the Paris train station scene looks familiar to first-time viewers of *Casablanca*, it's because the sets were used several weeks earlier in filming *Now, Voyager*. But this was not uncommon in the studio system days; it was one of the advantages of the system that the same material could be used over and over. The studio practiced another kind of deception during the final airport scene: The plane is a miniature, and the attendants surrounding it are midgets. This process enabled Curtiz to shoot on a soundstage, where he could control the fog and other conditions. It was also less expensive than shooting at night at a real airport with a real airplane.

The End

#6

There are probably dozens of reasons why Humphrey Bogart and Ingrid Bergman never made another movie together after *Casablanca*: they worked for different studios, Bogart's subsequent affair and marriage to Lauren Bacall, Bergman's subsequent affair, marriage, and exile to Italy. Still, those were not insurmountable. After all, director Roman Polanski is a wanted criminal in Los Angeles, and he still makes movies.

But perhaps the most important reason was that they never knew each other well enough to want to cut through the studio red tape and wade through the personal scheduling quagmires to make a second or third picture together. Their screen personas may have been memorable to the world, but apparently did very little for either of them. Bergman's quote is famous: "I kissed Humphrey Bogart, but I never knew him."

And Bogart never really understood her, either. In 1954, when he was in Italy to make *Beat the Devil*, he saw Bergman for the first time in several years.

"We had supper together with other friends and he was a little bit upset about my having left Hollywood," Bergman said more than twenty years later. "He felt sorry for me because he had thought I had ruined my career by stepping away from the Hollywood scene and into Italian movies."

In 1954, remember, Bergman had already left her husband and

146

career for Roberto Rossellini. The scandal had made her one of the most ostracized women in the United States. Bogart's reputation for honesty (or tactlessness) is well-deserved if he actually upbraided Bergman—whom he didn't know all that well—instead of giving her the benefit of the doubt.

Because, said Bergman: "I said to him, 'I am a happy woman and maybe that is just as important as being a box office success in America.'"

What Bogart never realized is that Bergman's exile would soon end, and that her post-Italian career would include three Academy Award nominations and two Oscars. Like Bogart, she would eventually combine boxoffice success with personal happiness.

And, of course, each of them would always have *Casablanca*.

"Friends here in New York, where you very often have *Casablanca* on television, tell me they have seen it eight times and each time they plan to watch only a little bit of it," Bergman said in the same interview. "And then they get stuck and look at the whole thing again. People just can't turn it off!"

Index

A

Abbott and Costello, 6
Across the Pacific, 37, 53
Adam Had Four Sons, 37
Adventures of Robin Hood, The, 51-52, 58, 129
African Queen, The, 42, 103
After The Thin Man, 111
Agee, James, 89, 137
Albuquerque, Joao Luis, 132
Algiers, 39, 90, 93, 107
Alison, Joan, 22, 80, 88, 90
Allen, Woody, 91, 121, 122, 123, 124, 132
Altman, Robert, 42
Always a Bridesmaid, Never a Mother, 137
Anastasia, 48
Anderson, Judith, 45
Anderson, Maxwell, 45, 113
Angels with Dirty Faces, 30, 36, 58
Anne of a Thousand Days, 62
Annie Hall, 121
Anobile, Richard J., 136
Another Thin Man, 111
Anthony Adverse, 51
Archer, Eugene, 99
Arch of Triumph, 36

Arkin, Alan, 116
Around the World in Eighty Days, 102
Arsenic and Old Lace, 7, 52
Arthur, Jean, 102
Astor, Mary, 88, 124
Aumont, Jean-Pierre, 39

B

Bacall, Lauren, 9, 20, 44, 49, 113, 122, 136, 140, 141, 145
Background to Danger, 27, 30, 31
Back to the Future, 38
Bacon, Lloyd, 36
Bad Men of Missouri, 34, 38
Bananas, 91
Barnes, Howard, 109
Barry, Philip, 83
Barrymore, Ethel, 25
Barrymore, John, 25-26
Barrymore, Lionel, 25, 113
Battle Circus, 37
Beat the Devil, 98, 104, 145
Beatty, Warren, 102
Becket, 63
Behlmer, Rudy, 38, 72, 78, 137, 141
Bells of St. Mary's, The, 37

Belmondo, Jean-Paul, 133
Benchley, Nathaniel, 141
Benchley, Robert, 141
Ben-Hur, 62
Bergman, Ingmar, 97
Bergman, Ingrid, 4-6, 7, 8, 9, 10, 12, 13, 17, 21, 23, 24, 36, 39, 46-49, 51, 56, 62, 74, 75, 93, 98, 102, 104, 105, 122, 136, 142, 145, 146-147
Berkeley, Busby, 31
Best Years of Our Lives, The, 62
Birds, The, 106
Body Heat, 108
Bogart, Belmont DeForest, 44
Bogart, Humphrey, 1, 9, 10, 12, 20, 21, 23, 24-25, 26, 28, 30, 32, 34, 35, 36, 37, 38, 39, 42-46, 49, 53, 56, 62, 65, 74, 75, 88, 93, 98, 102-103, 104, 105, 108, 112, 113, 118, 122, 124, 127, 137, 140, 141, 145, 147
Bogdanovich, Peter, 142
Bogie, 100
Bonnie and Clyde, 102
Boyer, Charles, 36
Brady, Bill, 45

Brady, William, 45
Brand, Max, 118
Brando, Marlon, 103
Brazzaville, 118
Breathless, 133
Brennan, Walter, 113
Bronson, Charles, 117
Brother Orchid, 36-37
Buckner, Robert, 70, 93
Burgess, Alan, 142
Burnett, Murray, 22, 80,
  88, 90, 91-92, 128
Burnett, W. R., 31
Busch, Niven, 7

C

*Cabinet of Dr. Caligari,
  The,* 56
Caboblanco, 117
Cactus Flower, 37
Cagney, James, 27, 30,
  38, 70
Caine Mutiny, The, 46
Capa, Robert, 46
Capra, Frank, 7, 51, 52,
  58, 72
Captain Blood, 60
Carpenter, Elliott, 61
Cavett, Dick, 98
Chain Lightning, 37
Chandler, Raymond, 24,
  42, 66, 67, 132
*Charge of the Light
  Brigade, The,* 60
Chasen, Dave, 43
Cheap Detective, The,
  121
Cheyenne, 125
*Christmas in
  Connecticut,* 53
Churchill, Winston, 107,
  109
Citizen Kane, 24, 96, 97,
  102, 133
Coburn, Charles, 51,
  102, 104
Coffee, Lenore, 74
Cohan, George M., 70
Comancheros, The, 61
Committee, The, 87
Conflict, 37
Connery, Sean, 20
Conspirators, The, 53,
  54-55
Cool Hand Luke, 102

Cooper, Gary, 8, 32, 46,
  98
Corliss, Richard, 71, 96,
  134
Cotten, Joseph, 39
Crosby, Bing, 61
Crothers, Scatman, 126,
  127
Crowther, Bosley, 109
Cukor, George, 58
Curtiz, Michael, 9, 11,
  12, 21, 23, 36, 38,
  39, 51, 55-60, 61,
  62, 65, 71, 74, 75, 77,
  78, 80, 86, 87, 90,
  93, 105, 108, 129,
  137, 142, 144, 145

D

Dalio, Marcel, 124
Dark City, 63
Dark Victory, 30
Daughters Courageous,
  86
Daves, Delmer, 58
Davies, Joseph, 86
Davis, Bette, 30, 32, 34,
  49, 51, 60
Day at the Races, A, 91
Dead End, 34
Deadline USA, 37
Dead Ringer, 49
de Gaulle, Charles, 25,
  135
de Havilland, Olivia, 8,
  20, 52
*Demetrius and the
  Gladiators,* 58
Der Spion (The Spy), 56
Dietrich, Marlene, 108
Dirty Dozen, The, 67
Dirty Harry, 61
Donat, Robert, 50
Dorn, Philip, 39, 40
Double Indemnity, 35
Dr. Jekyll and Mr. Hyde,
  4, 37

E

Ebert, Roger, 96, 129
Elizondo, Hector, 126
Elliott, Paul, 128

Epstein, Julius J., 7, 8,
  12, 21, 67, 70, 71-72,
  74-79, 83, 86, 91,
  93, 96, 99, 104,
  105, 110, 136, 142,
  144
Epstein, Philip G., 7, 8,
  12, 21, 67, 70, 71-72,
  74, 75, 79, 83, 86,
  96, 105, 110, 142,
  144
Esmond, Carl, 39
*Everybody Comes to
  Rick's,* 22-23, 25, 71,
  78, 88, 92, 107, 110,
  128, 133, 141, 144
Everybody's Welcome,
  21

F

Falk, Peter, 121
Fanny, 83
Farber, Manny, 105, 109
Faulkner, William, 66,
  113, 139
Faust, Frederick, 118
Finney, Albert, 121
Fitzgerald, Ella, 42
Fitzgerald, F. Scott, 66
Flash Gordon, 118
Fleming, Victor, 4
Flynn, Errol, 25, 26, 38,
  52, 60, 72
Fontanne, Lynn, 53
Ford, John, 58, 60
For Whom the Bell Tolls,
  8, 13, 48, 102, 104
Four Daughters, 74, 83
Fox, Michael J., 38
Francisco, Charles, 141
Friday the 13th, 111
Friedrich, Otto, 139, 140
Front Page, The, 111
Furthman, Jules, 113

G

Gable, Clark, 32, 98
Garfield, John, 35, 86
Garson, Greer, 50
Gaslight, 36
Gehman, Richard, 30
Georges, Trevor Michael,
  128
Gibson, Mel, 113, 116
Glaser, Paul Michael,
  124

Godard, Jean-Luc, 97, 132
Godfather III, 16-17
Goebbels, Joseph, 57
Goldwyn, Sam, 60
Gone With the Wind, 4, 7, 24, 67, 96, 129, 133
Goodbye, Mr. Chips, 50
Goodman, Ezra, 141
Goodman, Walter, 87
Gordon, Ruth, 45
Gould, Elliot, 42
Graduate, The, 102
Grand Hotel, 110
Grant, Cary, 7, 32, 98, 111
Grantham, Leslie, 128
Grapes of Wrath, The, 67
Greenberg, Harvey, 108
Greenstreet, Sidney, 21, 37, 52, 53, 56, 100, 105, 121, 142
Guess Who's Coming to Dinner, 102
Gumshoe, 121

H
Halliwell, Leslie, 96
Hamilton, Ian, 144
Hammett, Dashiell, 34, 66, 67, 111
Harmetz, Ajean, 80
Haun, Harry, 71
Havana, 113, 117
Haver, Ronald, 72, 137, 141
Hawks, Howard, 58, 60, 86, 112, 113
Hayworth, Rita, 39
Hecht, Ben, 67, 111
Hemingway, Ernest, 8, 107
Henreid, Paul, 12, 21, 25, 26, 31, 39, 49-50, 53, 56, 61, 65, 75-77, 93, 105, 113, 142
Hepburn, Audrey, 9
Heston, Charlton, 27, 63, 97
Higgins, Bertie, 122
Higham, Charles, 97
Highlander 2: The Quickening, 20

High Sierra, 30, 31, 32, 43
His Girl Friday, 111
Hitchcock, Alfred, 4, 48, 51, 58, 60, 106
Hoffman, Dustin, 102
Holiday Inn, 61
Hopkins, Arthur, 45
Horne, Lena, 41, 42
Houge, Peter, 106
House Calls, 7
Howard, Leslie, 4, 30, 45-46
Howard, Peter, 87
Humphrey, Maude, 44
Hupfeld, Herman, 21
Huston, John, 31, 32, 34, 49, 52, 53, 86, 87, 113
Huston, Walter, 87
Huxley, Aldous, 66
Hyams, Joe, 141, 145

I
In a Lonely Place, 46
Inn of the Sixth Happiness, The, 37
Intermezzo, 4
In the Heat of the Night, 102
Invasion of the Body Snatchers, 61
Invisible Man, The, 51
Isle of Fury, 30

J
Jagger, Dean, 39
James, Henry, 106
Jerome, M. K., 138
Jezebel, 32
Johnson, Nunnally, 67
Jones, Jennifer, 104
Joseph, Edmund, 70
Julia, Raul, 113, 116

K
Kael, Pauline, 58, 105-106
Karnot, Stephen, 88, 89
Kaye, Danny, 61
Keaton, Diane, 121
Keighley, William, 58
Kelly, Gene, 49
Key Largo, 113, 114-15, 122
Kid Creole, 61

Kid Galahad, 30, 36
Kings Row, 125
Kinskey, Leonid, 21
Kline, Wally, 72
Koch, Howard, 12, 21, 71, 72, 74-80, 86-87, 90, 91, 142-44

L
Lacy, Jerry, 100, 122
Ladd, Alan, 132
Lamarr, Hedy, 39, 41, 54, 56, 132
Lang, Fritz, 52
Last of the Comanches, 112
Lawrence of Arabia, 51
Leamer, Laurence, 142
Lean, David, 51
LeBeau, Madeline, 61
Leigh, Vivien, 5
Leroy, Mervyn, 51
Letter, The, 86
Letter From an Unknown Woman, 86
Life of Emile Zola, The, 64
Lindstrom, Peter, 48
Liotta, Ray, 126
Little Caesar, 27, 62
Loder, John, 132
Long Goodbye, The, 42
Lord, Robert, 110
Lorre, Peter, 21, 25-26, 35, 52-53, 56, 61, 105, 142
Loy, Myrna, 111
Lukas, Paul, 102
Lunt, Alfred, 53
Lupino, Ida, 32, 49

M
M, 52
MacArthur, Charles, 111
MacGuffin, 60
MacMurray, Fred, 35
Maltese Falcon, The, 12, 24, 34, 52, 53, 75, 124
Maltin, Leonard, 96, 140
Maltz, Albert, 76, 78
Man Called Bogart, A, 126, 136
Manhattan, 121
Man with Bogart's Face, The, 100

Man Who Came to Dinner, The, 83
Marx, Groucho, 90-91
Mask of Dimitrios, The, 52
Matter of Time, A, 36
Mayer, Louis B., 17, 39, 64
Mayer, Roger, 132
McCarty, Clifford, 137
McGraw, Charles, 124, 125
McKenzie, Aeneas, 72, 110
Mellen, Joan, 106
Men Are Such Fools, 31
Methot, Mayo, 9, 12, 24, 44, 127
Mildred Pierce, 60
Milian, Tomas, 116
Minnelli, Vincente, 36, 58
Mission to Moscow, 86, 87, 144
Mister Roberts, 27
Mitchum, Robert, 42
Moon of Israel, 60
Moran, Dolores, 113
More the Merrier, The, 102, 104
Morgan, Dennis, 38-39, 40
Morocco, 108
Moyers, Bill, 92
Mr. Moto, 52
Mr. Skeffington, 83
Mr. Smith Goes to Washington, 51, 52
Muni, Paul, 64
Murder on the Orient Express, 49
Murphy, Eddie, 20
Muse, Clarence, 42

N
Nazi Agent, 56
Negulesco, Jean, 56, 86
Newman, Alfred, 104
Newman, Paul, 102
Night and Day, 91
Night at the Opera, 91
Night in Casablanca, A, 90
Niven, David, 60
Notorious, 51
Now, Voyager, 145

O
O'Connor, Kevin, 100
O'Hara, Maureen, 49
Oklahoma Kid, The, 38
Olin, Lena, 116, 117
Orry-Kelly, 62
Ophuls, Max, 86
Out of the Past, 42

P
Page, Joy, 21
Paris, Barry, 58, 142
Parker, Dorothy, 66
Parker, Eleanor, 87
Parker, Robert, 38
Passage to Marseille, 36, 37, 61, 100
Perelman, S. J., 66
Pete 'n' Tillie, 83
Petrified Forest, The, 30, 42, 45, 46
Pfeiffer, Michelle, 113, 116
Philadelphia Story, The, 83
Play It Again, Sam, 100, 120-21, 123, 132
Pleshette, Suzanne, 106
Poitier, Sidney, 102
Polanski, Roman, 145
Police Academy, 111
Pollack, Sydney, 116
Powell, William, 111
Presley, Elvis, 61, 63
Pride of the Marines, 64

Q
Quinn, Anthony, 136
Quirk, Lawrence J., 46

R
Raft, George, 27, 29, 30-31, 32, 34-35, 38, 40
Rage in Heaven, 4
Rains, Claude, 21, 25, 49, 50-52, 83, 86, 102, 103-4, 113, 118, 142
Random Harvest, 39
Rapper, Irving, 142
Rascoe, Judith, 116
Rathbone, Basil, 52
Rayfiel, David, 116
Reagan, Ronald, 38, 39, 40

Redford, Robert, 116, 117
Reinhardt, Max, 50, 56
Return of Dr. X, The, 20, 136
Reuben, Reuben, 7, 83
Rey, Fernando, 117
Reynolds, Burt, 111
Rick's Bar Casablanca, 128
Roaring Twenties, The, 30
Robards, Jason, 117
Roberts, Tony, 121
Robin Hood, 58
Robinson, Casey, 39, 71, 75, 77, 78-79, 80, 90, 105, 144
Robinson, Edward G., 9, 27, 30, 36, 46, 113
Rocky, 111
Roosevelt, Franklin Delano, 86, 106-7, 109
Rosenzweig, Sidney, 108, 142
Ross, Chuck, 133, 134
Ross, Herbert, 122, 124
Rossellini, Isabella, 36, 48
Rossellini, Robertino, 48
Rossellini, Roberto, 48, 147
Russell, Kurt, 113, 116
Russell, Rosalind, 111
Rydell, Mark, 116

S
Sabrina, 9, 46
Sacchi, Robert, 100
Sahara, 74, 112
Sakall, S. Z., 21
Salinger, J. D., 144
Sanda, Dominique, 117
Sarris, Andrew, 58, 105
Scarface, 27
Schickel, Richard, 58
Schmidt, Lars, 48
Scholl, Jack, 138
Sea Hawk, The, 58
Sea Wolf, The, 35
Selznick, David O., 4-6, 7, 8, 13, 17, 39, 48, 62, 76, 104
Sennett, Ted, 142
Sergeant York, 32, 86

Seymour, Dan, 113, 125
Shadow of The Thin Man, 111
Sheridan, Ann, 27, 29, 38, 39, 41
Sherman, Vincent, 58, 144
Sherwood, Robert, 45
Shoot the Piano Player, 42
Siegel, Don, 61
Silk Stockings, 52
Singin' in the Rain, 24
Sirocco, 37, 100
Smith, Greg, 128
Song of Bernadette, The, 70, 104
Song of The Thin Man, 111
Sons of Katie Elder, The, 63
Soul, David, 124, 125, 126, 127
Soylent Green, 27
Spanish Main, 49
Stalin, Joseph, 86-87
Starsky and Hutch, 124
Steiger, Rod, 102
Steiner, Max, 12, 23, 64, 104
Stephani, Frederick, 118, 119, 120
Stevens, George, 102
Stone, Oliver, 20
Strawberry Blonde, The, 39
Streetcar Named Desire, 103
Summer, P. M., 132
Suspects, 108
Switching Channels, 111, 112

T
Tequila Sunrise, 113, 116
They Died With Their Boots On, 38, 60, 72
They Drive By Night, 27, 37
Thief of Baghdad, 56
Thief of Damascus, 49
Thin Man, The, 67, 111
Thin Man Goes Home, The, 111
Thomas, J. Parnell, 87

Thompson, J. Lee, 117
Thompson, Shelley, 128
Thomson, David, 108
Three Strangers, 52
To Have and Have Not, 60, 100, 112, 122
Total Recall, 16
Touch of Evil, 97
Toumanova, Tamara, 39
Tracy, Spencer, 4, 46, 98, 102
Treasure of the Sierra Madre, The, 37, 46
Trilling, Steve, 42
Truffaut, Francois, 42, 132, 133
Turner, Ted, 129
Turner, Kathleen, 108, 111
Turner, Lana, 4
227, 121
Two Against the World, 30

U
Under Capricorn, 48
Urich, Robert, 38

V
Veidt, Conrad, 21, 50, 56-57, 61, 109, 113
Vidor, King, 58
Virginia City, 36

W
Wald, Jerry, 86, 91
Wallis, Hal, 6, 7-8, 9, 12, 13, 21, 30, 38, 39, 42, 50, 61, 62-65, 71, 72, 74-80, 90, 93, 109, 110, 142, 144
Walsh, Raoul, 31, 58
Warner, Albert, 64
Warner, Harry, 60, 64
Warner, Jack, 7, 8, 31, 34, 38, 64, 65, 72, 86, 87, 90, 93, 109, 144
Warner, Samuel, 64
Watch on the Rhine, 102
Wayne, John, 61, 63
Welles, Orson, 86, 97
Wellman, William, 58
We're No Angels, 36, 100
West, Nathanael, 66, 70

Weygand, Maxim, 25, 135
White Christmas, 61
White Heat, 27
Why We Fight, 72
Williams, Esther, 3
Williams, Frances, 21
Wilson, Dooley, 21, 39, 42, 61, 64, 96, 113, 129, 133
Wodehouse, P. G., 83
Wolper, David L., 124, 125-26, 132
Woolcott, Alexander, 45
Wyler, William, 62, 86
Wyman, Jane, 39

Y
Yankee Doodle Dandy, 27, 58, 61, 70, 71, 83, 93
Young, Gig, 124

Z
Zanuck, Darryl, 62, 64
Zolotow, Maurice, 96, 144
Zorina, Vera, 8-9